An Analysis of

Amos Tversky and Daniel Kahneman's

Judgment under Uncertainty
Heuristics and Biases

Camille Morvan
with
William J. Jenkins

Published by Macat International Ltd
24:13 Coda Centre, 189 Munster Road, London SW6 6AW.

Distributed exclusively by Routledge
2 Park Square, Milton Park, Abingdon, Oxon OX14 4RN
711 Third Avenue, New York, NY 10017, USA

Routledge is an imprint of the Taylor & Francis Group, an informa business

Copyright © 2017 by Macat International Ltd
Macat International has asserted its right under the Copyright, Designs and Patents Act
1988 to be identified as the copyright holder of this work.

The print publication is protected by copyright. Prior to any prohibited reproduction, storage in
a retrieval system, distribution or transmission in any form or by any means, electronic, mechanical, recording or otherwise, permission should be obtained from the publisher or where
applicable a license permitting restricted copying in the United Kingdom should be obtained
from the Copyright Licensing Agency Ltd, Barnard's Inn, 86 Fetter Lane, London EC4A 1EN, UK.

The ePublication is protected by copyright and must not be copied, reproduced, transferred,
distributed, leased, licensed or publicly performed or used in any way except as specifically
permitted in writing by the publishers, as allowed under the terms and conditions under which
it was purchased, or as strictly permitted by applicable copyright law. Any unauthorised distribution or use of this text may be a direct infringement of the authors and the publishers' rights
and those responsible may be liable in law accordingly.

www.macat.com
info@macat.com

Cataloguing in Publication Data
A catalogue record for this book is available from the British Library.
Library of Congress Cataloguing-in-Publication Data is available upon request.
Cover illustration: Etienne Gilfillan

ISBN 978-1-912303-68-7 (hardback)
ISBN 978-1-912128-94-5 (paperback)
ISBN 978-1-912282-56-2 (e-book)

Notice
The information in this book is designed to orientate readers of the work under analysis,
to elucidate and contextualise its key ideas and themes, and to aid in the development
of critical thinking skills. It is not meant to be used, nor should it be used, as a
substitute for original thinking or in place of original writing or research. References and
notes are provided for informational purposes and their presence does not constitute
endorsement of the information or opinions therein. This book is presented solely for
educational purposes. It is sold on the understanding that the publisher is not engaged
to provide any scholarly advice. The publisher has made every effort to ensure that
this book is accurate and up-to-date, but makes no warranties or representations with
regard to the completeness or reliability of the information it contains. The information
and the opinions provided herein are not guaranteed or warranted to produce particular
results and may not be suitable for students of every ability. The publisher shall not be
liable for any loss, damage or disruption arising from any errors or omissions, or from
the use of this book, including, but not limited to, special, incidental, consequential or
other damages caused, or alleged to have been caused, directly or indirectly, by the
information contained within.

CONTENTS

THE MACAT LIBRARY

The Macat Library is a series of unique academic explorations of seminal works in the humanities and social sciences – books and papers that have had a significant and widely recognised impact on their disciplines. It has been created to serve as much more than just a summary of what lies between the covers of a great book. It illuminates and explores the influences on, ideas of, and impact of that book. Our goal is to offer a learning resource that encourages critical thinking and fosters a better, deeper understanding of important ideas.

Each publication is divided into three Sections: Influences, Ideas, and Impact. Each Section has four Modules. These explore every important facet of the work, and the responses to it.

This Section-Module structure makes a Macat Library book easy to use, but it has another important feature. Because each Macat book is written to the same format, it is possible (and encouraged!) to cross-reference multiple Macat books along the same lines of inquiry or research. This allows the reader to open up interesting interdisciplinary pathways.

To further aid your reading, lists of glossary terms and people mentioned are included at the end of this book (these are indicated by an asterisk [*] throughout) – as well as a list of works cited.

Macat has worked with the University of Cambridge to identify the elements of critical thinking and understand the ways in which six different skills combine to enable effective thinking.
Three allow us to fully understand a problem; three more give us the tools to solve it. Together, these six skills make up the **PACIER** model of critical thinking. They are:

ANALYSIS – understanding how an argument is built
EVALUATION – exploring the strengths and weaknesses of an argument
INTERPRETATION – understanding issues of meaning

CREATIVE THINKING – coming up with new ideas and fresh connections
PROBLEM-SOLVING – producing strong solutions
REASONING – creating strong arguments

To find out more, visit **WWW.MACAT.COM.**

CRITICAL THINKING AND *"JUDGMENT UNDER UNCERTAINTY"*

Primary critical thinking skill: INTERPRETATION
Secondary critical thinking skill: ANALYSIS

Amos Tversky and Daniel Kahneman's 1974 paper 'Judgement Under Uncertainty: Heuristics and Biases' is a landmark in the history of psychology. Though a mere seven pages long, it has helped reshape the study of human rationality, and had a particular impact on economics – where Tversky and Kahneman's work helped shape the entirely new sub discipline of 'behavioral economics.'

The paper investigates human decision-making, specifically what human brains tend to do when we are forced to deal with uncertainty or complexity. Based on experiments carried out with volunteers, Tversky and Kahneman discovered that humans make predictable errors of judgement when forced to deal with ambiguous evidence or make challenging decisions. These errors stem from 'heuristics' and 'biases' – mental shortcuts and assumptions that allow us to make swift, automatic decisions, often usefully and correctly, but occasionally to our detriment.

The paper's huge influence is due in no small part to its masterful use of high-level interpretative and analytical skills – expressed in Tversky and Kahneman's concise and clear definitions of the basic heuristics and biases they discovered. Still providing the foundations of new work in the field 40 years later, the two psychologists' definitions are a model of how good interpretation underpins incisive critical thinking.

ABOUT THE AUTHORS OF THE ORIGINAL WORK

Israeli psychologist **Amos Tversky** was born in 1937 and was educated both in Israel and the United States. He attended the University of Michigan, where he was so respected by his peers that they came up with a mock intelligence test: the faster you realize Tversky is smarter than you, the smarter you are.

His colleague **Daniel Kahneman**, born in 1934, was likewise an Israeli psychologist. Both men did military service, where they developed new and improved ways of assessing personality for the Israeli army that sparked a long-term interest in human decision-making. After they met in 1968, Tversky and Kahneman went on to publish 24 academic papers together, transforming the study of decision-making in the process. Tversky died in 1996, but Kahneman won a Nobel Prize in 2002 for their joint work–and has lived long enough to see it become the focus of The Undoing Project, a bestseller by Michael Lewis.

ABOUT THE AUTHORS OF THE ANALYSIS

Dr Camille Morvan is a psychologist, researcher and founder of the psychological human resources company Goshaba. She has taught at Sciences Politiques in Paris and at Harvard University, as well as working at the Ecole normale supérieure.

Dr Bill Jenkins holds a PhD in psychology from the University of Michigan. He is currently co-chair of the Department of Psychology at Mercer University.

ABOUT MACAT

GREAT WORKS FOR CRITICAL THINKING

Macat is focused on making the ideas of the world's great thinkers accessible and comprehensible to everybody, everywhere, in ways that promote the development of enhanced critical thinking skills.

It works with leading academics from the world's top universities to produce new analyses that focus on the ideas and the impact of the most influential works ever written across a wide variety of academic disciplines. Each of the works that sit at the heart of its growing library is an enduring example of great thinking. But by setting them in context – and looking at the influences that shaped their authors, as well as the responses they provoked – Macat encourages readers to look at these classics and game-changers with fresh eyes. Readers learn to think, engage and challenge their ideas, rather than simply accepting them.

"Macat offers an amazing first-of-its-kind tool for interdisciplinary learning and research. Its focus on works that transformed their disciplines and its rigorous approach, drawing on the world's leading experts and educational institutions, opens up a world-class education to anyone."

Andreas Schleicher
Director for Education and Skills, Organisation for Economic Co-operation and Development

'Macat is taking on some of the major challenges in university education … They have drawn together a strong team of active academics who are producing teaching materials that are novel in the breadth of their approach.'

Prof Lord Broers,
former Vice-Chancellor of the University of Cambridge

'The Macat vision is exceptionally exciting. It focuses upon new modes of learning which analyse and explain seminal texts which have profoundly influenced world thinking and so social and economic development. It promotes the kind of critical thinking which is essential for any society and economy.
This is the learning of the future.'

Rt Hon Charles Clarke, former UK Secretary of State for Education

'The Macat analyses provide immediate access to the critical conversation surrounding the books that have shaped their respective discipline, which will make them an invaluable resource to all of those, students and teachers, working in the field.'

Professor William Tronzo, University of California at San Diego

WAYS IN TO THE TEXT

KEY POINTS

- Amos Tversky and Daniel Kahneman are Israeli psychologists.*

- Their article "Judgment under Uncertainty: Heuristics and Biases" (1974) reveals the mental processes that affect our judgment and decision-making at a subconscious* level— that is, the mental processes of which we are unaware.

- "Judgment under Uncertainty" revolutionized decision-making and economics.

Who Are Amos Tversky and Daniel Kahneman?

Amos Tversky (1937–96) and Daniel Kahneman (b. 1934), the authors of "Judgment under Uncertainty: Heuristics and Biases" (1974) are Israeli psychologists. Educated in Israel and in the United States, both spent time serving in the Israeli armed forces; Tversky was a paratroop captain cited for bravery after saving a man's life, Kahneman a military psychologist who assessed the capabilities of his fellow soldiers ("psychology" here referring to the study of the mind and how it affects behavior).

Their military experience sparked a long-term interest in human decision-making. Tversky suggested that growing up in a country fighting for its survival influenced him to think about applied, real-world judgment and decision-making, rather than about theoretical problems alone.

Both men married star psychologists: Tversky the American cognitive psychologist* Barbara Gans* and Kahneman the British psychologist Anne Treisman* (cognitive psychology is the study of the human mind and behavior as it relates to thought). Treisman would go on to conduct seminal experimental studies about attention and perception.

Tversky and Kahneman met in 1968. Their collaboration was both fruitful and unusual. As Kahneman explains in his biography, "I quickly discovered that Amos had a remedy for everything I found difficult about writing."[1] From 1971–2, they went to the Oregon Research Institute in Eugene, Oregon (an institution dedicated to research in psychology), a time that Kahneman describes as the most productive of his life.[2]

For their work together, Kahneman received the Nobel Memorial Prize in Economics in 2002. Tversky had died in 1996 from cancer; he would undoubtedly have shared the honor had he lived. Together they had paved the way to the completely new field of behavioral economics:* the application of scientific insights into human behavior to understand and predict people's economic decisions.

What Does *"Judgment under Uncertainty"* Say?

The paper changed the way scholars understand decision-making. It revealed the automatic (subconscious) influences that affect human judgment. Tversky and Kahneman showed that when the outcome of a decision is uncertain, our decision-making can be flawed. They went on to show that many of the errors we make are predictable—we all display similar automatic reactions in specific contexts.

These reactions are called heuristics:* mental shortcuts that help us to make decisions quickly and automatically. In some cases and situations, they help us to make correct decisions; in others they lead us to make errors. Once we know *how* the mental shortcuts prompt us to think, we know how they can cause problems in our thinking. That is why they are predictable.

To investigate the heuristics channeling our thought processes, Tversky and Kahneman devised a number of decision-making problems. In one experiment they asked participants to estimate the answer to the multiplication 8x7x6x5x4x3x2x1. They then asked another group to estimate the answer to the multiplication 1x2x3x4x5x6x7x8.

Look at the multiplications closely and you will see that they are the same. However, the estimate made by the first group was higher than the estimate made by the second group; why?

Tversky and Kahneman worked out that the differences between the group estimates could be attributed to the use of a heuristic. One of our mental shortcuts is to pay most attention to the first thing we see. So the first group saw two high numbers (8x7), while the second group saw two low numbers (1x2). This initial prompt led the first group to give a higher estimate than the second group.

This example shows two concepts that are at the core of Kahneman and Tversky's work: heuristics and bias.* As we have seen, heuristics are simple rules that the brain can use to take decisions. Their benefit is that they help us to make decisions quickly, instead of devoting our time and attention to reasoning carefully through the full problem. A cognitive* bias, on the other hand, is a systematic error in thinking. In the case of the multiplication task, the bias is caused by our automatic tendency to focus on the first bit of information we receive (either 8x7 or 1x2). When Tversky and Kahneman talk about bias they are talking about how we deviate from the "objectively right" or "correct" answer to a problem.

Tversky and Kahneman combined experimental research in psychology with theories of economics. Their work revolutionized both these fields by challenging the model of rational choice theory,* then popular across the social sciences. This theory assumes that humans are rational agents* (that we are capable of acting purely on the basis of rational thought) who, when faced with a decision, assess all their options and what the outcome of each option will be. We compare these options, the theory claims, and then choose the one that benefits us the most (or damages us the least).

For this model to work, anyone faced with a decision needs to know (in advance) all options open to them and the outcome of each option. This is unrealistic though—we cannot always know what the future will hold, and human cognition is limited. In fact, the capacity of our working memory is limited to around four pieces of information at any given time, which means that most people can only focus on a few items at once. Tversky and Kahneman's combination of psychology and economics challenged the rational agent model and provided an alternative view of how human decision-making actually works.

Why Does *"Judgment under Uncertainty"* Matter?

Before the text's publication, most practitioners and academics relied on the rational agent model to predict behavior, according to which humans make rational decisions. Although many authors pointed out that this was not realistic, it took Tversky and Kahneman's work to usher in a new way of approaching decision-making and human behavior. Their work has transformed all the fields concerned with human decision-making. These include political science (the study of political behavior and institutions), marketing, management, finance, public policy (the development and implementation of policies by national or regional government), and law.

As Tversky and Kahneman's ideas became mainstream, they transformed the popular conversation about decision-making. The emergence of related books for a general audience, several of which have been written by disciples or colleagues of Kahneman and Tversky, reflects the broad interest in the topic. The American Israeli psychologist Dan Ariely* wrote the best-selling book *Predictably Irrational* (2008); the American economist Steven Levitt* and the journalist Stephen Dubner* wrote *Freakonomics* (2005), which has sold more than 4 million copies worldwide. The American economist Richard Thaler* and legal scholar Cass Sunstein* wrote *Nudge* (2008), which brought home the importance of behavioral insights for those working in public policy.[3]

Tversky and Kahneman followed "Judgment under Uncertainty" with another article, "Prospect Theory: An Analysis of Decision under Risk" (1979). Prospect theory* is the theoretical counterpart of "Judgment under Uncertainty." Describing the way people make decisions when all the outcomes carry a risk, it helps us understand when and why we take risks, and when and why we play safe.[4] Both articles, which allow us to see for ourselves the flaws in our own judgments and help us to understand the decisions made by others, are essential reading for anyone interested in decision-making. We can also use this research to create better organizations and societies.

One way to improve society is by educating citizens to understand the limitations of reasoning. That is not to say that we can completely overcome those limitations, we are animals with finite cognitive resources. Many organizations and institutions could benefit from integrating what we understand about human decision-making, flaws and all.

NOTES

1   Daniel Kahneman, "Daniel Kahneman—Biographical," Nobelprize. org, accessed April 21, 2016, http://www.nobelprize.org/nobel_prizes/ economic-sciences/laureates/2002/kahneman-bio.html.

2   Kahneman, "Daniel Kahneman—Biographical."

3   Dan Ariely, *Predictably Irrational: The Hidden Forces That Shape Our Decisions* (New York: HarperCollins, 2009); Steven D. Levitt and Stephen J. Dubner, *Freakonomics: A Rogue Economist Explores the Hidden Side of Everything* (New York: William Morrow, 2006); and Richard H. Thaler and Cass R. Sunstein, *Nudge* (New Haven: Yale University Press, 2008).

4   Daniel Kahneman and Amos Tversky, "Prospect Theory: An Analysis of Decision under Risk," *Econometrica: Journal of the Econometric Society* 47, no. 2 (1979): 263–91.

SECTION 1
INFLUENCES

MODULE 1
THE AUTHORS AND THE
HISTORICAL CONTEXT

KEY POINTS

- Tversky and Kahneman's work laid the foundations for the field of behavioral economics* (the application of scientific insights into human behavior to the understanding of economic decisions) and was influential in both cognitive* and social psychology*—the study of the human mind with regard to thought and social behavior respectively.

- The authors' military backgrounds influenced their work by giving them a lifelong interest in how decisions are made under conditions of uncertainty.

- Both authors grew up in Israel, at a time when the country was fighting for its existence; this directly influenced their interest in how ordinary people make decisions.

Why Read This Text?

Amos Tversky and Daniel Kahneman's 1974 paper "Judgment under Uncertainty: Heuristics and Biases" is essential reading for anyone interested in decision-making. It made a significant contribution to psychology, economics, and the other social sciences* (the various disciplines concerned with understanding the forms and theory of social behavior). Its importance is reflected in the fact that it has been cited over 36,000 times—a remarkably high figure for a psychology article.[1]

Before the paper's publication, economists and social scientists tended to accept the assumption that humans are rational and always make considered decisions. As Kahneman wrote later, "Social scientists in the 1970s broadly accepted two ideas about human nature. First, people are generally rational, and their thinking is normally sound.

❝ I will never know if my vocation as a psychologist was a result of my early exposure to interesting gossip, or whether my interest in gossip was an indication of a budding vocation. Like many other Jews, I suppose, I grew up in a world that consisted exclusively of people and words, and most of the words were about people. ❞

Daniel Kahneman, "Daniel Kahneman—Biographical," *Nobelprize.org*

Second, emotions such as fear, affection, and hatred explain most of the occasions on which people depart from rationality. Our article challenged both assumptions without discussing them directly. We documented systematic errors in the thinking of normal people, and we traced these errors to the design of the machinery of cognition rather than to the corruption of thought by emotion."[2]

While other scholars had already questioned the idea of decision-making as a wholly rational process, Tversky and Kahneman's work had a particularly significant impact. Their success was partly due to timing (notably because of the evolution of the fields of economics and psychology) and partly to the novel and experimental way in which the paper was written. As part of their research they created numerous decision-making games for testing on people. This innovative approach was used to good effect in the article itself, which presented the reader with the same decision-making problems that it was examining. As a reader, you feel compelled to answer these; more often than not, your answer ends up being wrong. Tversky and Kahneman, then, demonstrate their argument as their article unfolds.

Authors' Lives

Daniel Kahneman's parents were Jewish. Originally from Lithuania, they moved to France, but Kahneman himself was born on a family visit to Tel Aviv in 1934. After World War II,* the family left France for good, moving to what is now Israel. This completely altered Kahneman's life experience. For the first time, he had friends and felt that he fitted in with his classmates.[3]

Kahneman attributes his interest in psychology to growing up in a Jewish community composed of fascinating, complex people. When he went to a career guidance session, psychology emerged at the top of the list of recommendations, with economics not far behind. He would go on to contribute to the emergence of a new field that combines psychology with economics: behavioral economics—a field in which scientific insights into human behavior are applied to the understanding and prediction of our economic decisions.

In 1954, after finishing his degree in psychology, Kahneman began working as a psychologist for the Israeli armed forces. Two years later, he finished his military service and received a grant to study for his PhD at the University of California, Berkeley. From then on his career would be split between the US and Israel.

Kahneman met Amos Tversky in 1968 at university in Jerusalem. Three years younger than Kahneman, Tversky was born in the city of Haifa and his mother was a member of the first Israeli Knesset* (parliament). He served as a paratroop captain in the Israeli armed forces before going to the University of Michigan to earn his PhD.

Tversky was a brilliant scholar. His peers thought so highly of him that they devised the "Tversky Intelligence Test." In this test, as described by the American psychologist Adam Alter,* "The faster you realized Tversky was smarter than you, the smarter you were."[4] Tversky died of cancer in 1996, aged just 59.

Authors' Background
During Kahneman's time in the military he worked as a psychologist, trying to predict which soldiers would be appropriate for different roles. This led to a lifelong interest in the psychology of prediction and led him to develop theories about how ordinary people forecast the

future. This became the basis for his collaboration with Tversky.

The fact that Kahneman started his career in Israel certainly influenced his life. Very early on in his career, he had responsibilities that he was unlikely to have been given elsewhere. In his acceptance speech for the Nobel Memorial Prize for Economic Sciences in 2002, he explained, "And if it appears odd that a twenty-one-year-old lieutenant would be asked to set up an interviewing system for an army, one should remember that the state of Israel and its institutions were only seven years old at the time, that improvisation was the norm, and that professionalism did not exist. [With] a BA in the appropriate field, I was the best-trained professional psychologist in the military."[5]

Tversky, for his part, suggested that "growing up in a country that's fighting for survival, you're perhaps more likely to think simultaneously about applied and theoretical problems."[6] Their meeting in 1968 kick-started a lively discussion about decision-making and probability estimation* (in which people are asked to estimate the likelihood of something based on some evidence they see or hear).

Their collaboration was intense and unusual. Kahneman reports in his biography that he had enjoyed collaborative work before, but that this was "something different."[7] From 1971–2, Kahneman and Tversky went to the Oregon Research Institute in Eugene, Oregon (an institution noted for its contribution to the field of psychology). Kahneman refers to this year as the most productive of his life. After their return to Israel, they wrote a paper to summarize their collaborative work on decision-making. "Judgment under Uncertainty" was born.

NOTES

1   Google Scholar, "Judgment under Uncertainty," accessed April 21, 2016, https://scholar.google.com/citations?view_op=view_citation&hl=en&user=9puL9pAAAAAJ&citation_for_view=9puL9pAAAAAJ:u-x6o8ySG0sC.

2   Daniel Kahneman, *Thinking, Fast and Slow* (New York: Farrar, Strauss and Giroux, 2011), 8.

3   Daniel Kahneman, "Daniel Kahneman—Biographical," Nobelprize.org, accessed April 21, 2016, http://www.nobelprize.org/nobel_prizes/economic-sciences/laureates/2002/kahneman-bio.html.

4   Malcolm Gladwell, *David and Goliath: Underdogs, Misfits, and the Art of Battling Giants* (Boston: Little, Brown and Company, 2013).

5   Kahneman, "Daniel Kahneman—Biographical."

6   Kevin McKean, "Decisions: Games Minds Play," *Chicago Tribune*, June 23, 1985, accessed April 21, 2016, http://articles.chicagotribune.com/1985-06-23/features/8502100242_1_route-soldiers-answers.

7   Kahneman, "Daniel Kahneman—Biographical."

MODULE 2
ACADEMIC CONTEXT

KEY POINTS

- The paper "Judgment under Uncertainty" describes how we make decisions when we don't have all the relevant information.

- When Tversky and Kahneman were writing, the dominant belief in the social sciences* was that humans make decisions that maximize the things they value on inherently rational principles.

- Kahneman and Tversky used experiments to study decision-making. By systematically comparing the results of many experiments, they could show that humans regularly deviate from the rational agent model* (a "rational agent" being someone who is always capable of computing the outcomes of any decision in order to choose the most beneficial option).

The Work in its Context

Amos Tversky and Daniel Kahneman's paper "Judgment under Uncertainty: Heuristics and Biases" challenged orthodox economic thinking using the latest psychological* developments. Their work questioned one of the basic tenets of neoclassical economic theory*— the rational agent model.

Founded in the 1860s, the neoclassical economic theory is an approach to economic behavior founded on the principle that economic decisions are made according to rational considerations about how we might benefit from them. Until this point, the dominant economical model was based on the principle that only "real" values—concerning things such as labor, the scarcity of a good, and so on—had an impact on

❝ Any discussion of the modern history of research on everyday judgment must take note of the large shadow cast by the classical model of rational choice. ❞

Thomas Gilovich et al., *Heuristics and Biases: The Psychology of Intuitive Judgment*

the economy. Comparatively, the neoclassical model acknowledged the importance of *subjective* value. For example, the price people are willing to pay for something does not depend on how difficult it is to produce, but on the subjective satisfaction they think they will get out of it.

Economists, however, did not formalize how these subjective values were used. They assumed that we use them rationally, and that we incorporate the subjective value of a good or service into our decision-making. The resulting rational agent model emerged within the field of economics, but strongly influenced all the social sciences, as well as medicine and law.

Social scientists generally studied decision-making from one of two perspectives:

• Descriptively* (the actual decisions people make or have made).
• Normatively* (the decisions people should make).

By the 1970s, researchers broadly accepted that people are usually rational and that their thinking is normally sound. There was also broad agreement that most of the occasions on which people depart from rationality can be explained by emotions such as fear, affection, and hatred.1

At that time, the dominant model in psychology was a set of theories and analogies that conceptualized the mind as a computer. This was particularly useful for Tversky and Kahneman's work. It equipped them with the mathematical tools needed to compare psychological results with the formal predictions of the rational agent model.

Overview of the Field

Prior to Tversky and Kahneman, three important publications departed from the rational model, laying the groundwork for "Judgment under Uncertainty." One was empirical,* one methodological,* and one theoretical.[2]

Empirically (that is, using evidence verifiable by observation), the American psychologist Paul Meehl* looked at predictions made by medical experts, in which doctors combine data informally "in their head" to reach a diagnosis. He compared these with predictions made by a mechanical prediction tool created for a similar diagnostic purpose. This used algorithms and other mathematical tools. The mechanical predictions always outperformed the experts' ones.[2]

Methodologically (that is, through the use of a specific process designed to shed light on a research subject), the American psychologist Ward Edwards* introduced the concept of Bayesian analysis*—a method of calculating the probability of different outcomes.[3] Edwards's research[4] showed that there was a difference between what people thought was the best solution to a problem and what turned out to be the "ideal" solution. As a result, many researchers turned their attention to the causes of this discord.

In the theoretical realm, finally, the American political scientist and social scientist Herbert Simon* began to use the term "heuristic"* in a positive sense in the 1950s. He was aware that decision-makers do not have the time and mental capacity to consider all the factors involved, as described by the rational agent model. Instead, he argued, humans use heuristics—mental shortcuts—to cope effectively with their cognitive* limitations. He calls our limitations "bounded rationality;"* for him, our use of heuristics means that while human judgment is not perfect, it is satisfactory.

Academic Influences

One of Kahneman's earliest influences when he was an undergraduate at the Hebrew University of Jerusalem was the German American psychologist Kurt Lewin,* who introduced a three-step model of change to explore when and how individuals alter their behavior. At its most simplistic, this is labeled "Unfreeze. Change. Freeze." We get ready for change; we change; finally we consolidate the change.[5]

At Berkeley, Kahneman learned about vision and perception from the American psychologists Richard Lazarus* and Tom Cornsweet,*and developed a theory of attention as a limited resource with the Hungarian-born psychologist David Rapaport.*

Meanwhile, Tversky conducted his PhD at the University of Michigan. While working on his dissertation, he began collaborative research on measurement theory* (the theoretical understanding of how best to measure and quantify behavior). During this time he also met and collaborated with three American psychologists interested in the topic of decision-making: Ward Edwards,* Sarah Lichtenstein,*and Paul Slovic.* Of these, the most significant influence on Tversky's work was Edwards, with his studies of how people estimate probability. Edwards's work became the starting point for Tversky and Kahneman's research into heuristics and biases.

Tversky and Kahneman had a strong background in the use of experimental methods to study decision-making, and were also experts on perception. They knew that the brain has limited resources and they knew how to study these limitations. They used this background to approach the study of decision-making from a new angle.

NOTES

1   Daniel Kahneman, *Thinking, Fast and Slow* (New York: Farrar, Strauss and Giroux, 2011).

2   Paul E. Meehl, *Clinical Versus Statistical Prediction: A Theoretical Analysis and a Review of the Evidence* (Minneapolis: University of Minnesota Press, 1954).

3   Ward Edwards, "The Theory of Decision Making," *Psychological Bulletin* 51, no. 4 (1954): 380; and Ward Edwards et al., "Bayesian Statistical Inference for Psychological Research," *Psychological Review* 70, no. 3 (1963): 193.

4   Ward Edwards, "Conservatism in Human Information Processing," in *Formal Representation of Human Judgment*, ed. Benjamin Kleinmuntz (New York: John Wiley and Sons, 1968), 51.

5   Daniel Kahneman, "Daniel Kahneman—Biographical," Nobelprize.org, accessed April 21, 2016, http://www.nobelprize.org/nobel_prizes/economic-sciences/laureates/2002/kahneman-bio.html.

MODULE 3
THE PROBLEM

KEY POINTS

- Before "Judgment under Uncertainty," the dominant model of human decision-making was the rational agent model,* which underpinned the neoclassical model* of economics (a theory of economic behavior founded on the idea that economic decisions are made according to a rational and complete analysis of how we might benefit from those decisions).

- Researchers working before Tversky and Kahneman had pointed out that the rational agent model did not account for actual human decision-making; they highlighted the importance of human psychology* and cognitive* limitations.

- Tversky and Kahneman critiqued the rational agent model by demonstrating the flaws in human decision-making.

Core Question

In "Judgment under Uncertainty: Heuristics and Biases," Amos Tversky and Daniel Kahneman focus on how an individual makes decisions when the outcome is not certain. The dominant model for decision-making at the time was the rational agent model, according to which decision-makers have a perfect understanding of the value or satisfaction to be derived from each option. With that understanding they accurately assess each outcome before choosing the one that brings them the maximum benefit.

The problem is that this process requires unlimited cognitive capacities, but the cognitive capacity of humans is limited: we have limited attention, memory, capacity to carry out complicated calculations, and so on. So why was the rational agent model so widespread despite its unrealistic assertions?

66 If we had intended the article as a challenge to the
rational model, we would have written it differently,
and the challenge would have been less effective ...
The result would have been less crisp, less provocative,
and ultimately less defensible. As it was, we offered
a progress report on our study of judgment under
uncertainty, which included much solid evidence. All
inferences about human rationality were drawn by the
readers themselves. **99**

Daniel Kahneman, "Daniel Kahneman—Biographical," *Nobelprize.org*

The answer is that it was a practical tool to study what individuals
or groups might do, and it gave researchers a way of studying the
economy. In economics, the perfectly rational individual envisaged
by the theory is called "homo economicus."* Several authors
before Tversky and Kahneman agreed that homo economicus was
not realistic, and that the rational agent model was not satisfactory.
There were, however, no commonly accepted alternative models. In
"Judgment under Uncertainty," Tversky and Kahneman provided
an overview of how decisions are actually made. They provided
compelling evidence for the fact that human decisions often deviate
from the predictions of the rational agent model.

The Participants

The debate about the validity of the rational agent model in
understanding decision-making involved both economists and
psychologists. Influential economists, among them the French thinker
Maurice Allais* and the American social scientist Herbert Simon,*
questioned the model's limits and soundness.

The American scholar Ward Edwards* was one of the first
psychologists to bring economic models to psychology and use them

as a benchmark for contrasting human performance. Edwards researched how people make decisions, and whether decision-making can be improved through training. His paper "Behavioral Decision Theory" (1961) in the *Annual Review of Psychology*[1] proved so influential it brought about the formation of the new field of behavioral economics*—a field specifically concerned with the psychological, cognitive, and emotional factors informing individual economic decisions.[2]

Another psychologist in the debate was the American Paul Meehl.* Meehl showed that clinical decisions made by experts contain more errors than those based on statistics. In other words, if you give the same information to a computer program and a doctor, you will find that a well-programmed computer makes more accurate diagnoses than the doctor.[3] This finding gave Kahneman the idea of comparing human judgments with mathematical benchmarks.

The Contemporary Debate

The debate about rationality and choice was at its most fierce in the field of economics. While rational agent theorists did not claim that the theory can give a perfect account of how we make decisions, they did argue that the model was useful for predicting and comparing the outcome and pattern of choices. So the question became: "How far can we push the rational agent model?"

Critics of rational choice argued for a cautious approach to the model. The influential English economist John Maynard Keynes* was always very wary as to how far the model could be pushed. In 1953 the French psychologist Maurice Allais warned that the mathematical formalism of economics literature hid many key psychological constraints that affect decision-making, emphasizing the role of psychology: "What an individual considers in a random choice is not the monetary value of a gain but the psychological value attached to that gain."[4]

Two years later, in 1955, the political scientist and economist

Herbert Simon* pointed out that the human decision–making process is limited and, as a result, the rational model of choice is unrealistic.[5]

However, other thinkers had different ideas. The hugely influential American economist Milton Friedman* questioned the theoretical approach of Keynes and revived the rational agent model.[6] Paul Krugman,* a Nobel Prize*–winning American economist, wrote of Friedman's legacy, "But was it really a good idea to diminish the role of Economic Man that much? No, said Friedman, who argued in his 1953 essay 'The Methodology of Positive Economics' that economic theories should be judged not by their psychological realism but by their ability to predict behavior. And Friedman's two greatest triumphs as an economic theorist came from applying the hypothesis of rational behavior to questions other economists had thought beyond its reach."[7]

NOTES

1   Ward Edwards, "Behavioral Decision Theory," *Annual Review of Psychology* 12, no. 1 (1961): 473–98.

2   Lawrence D. Phillips and Detlof von Winterfeldt, "Reflections on the Contributions of Ward Edwards to Decision Analysis and Behavioral Research," in *Advances in Decision Analysis*, eds. W. Edwards et al. (London: Cambridge University Press, 2007), 71–80.

3   Paul E. Meehl, *Clinical Versus Statistical Prediction: A Theoretical Analysis and a Review of the Evidence* (Minneapolis: University of Minnesota Press, 1954).

4   Maurice Allais, "Le comportement de l'homme rationnel devant le risque: critique des postulats et axiomes de l'école américaine," *Econometrica: Journal of the Econometric Society* 21, no. 4 (1953): 503–46.

5   Herbert A. Simon, "A Behavioral Model of Rational Choice," *Quarterly Journal of Economics* 69, no. 1 (1955): 99–118.

6   Jonah Lehrer, "Milton Friedman and the Rational-Agent Model," *Science Blogs*, January 29, 2007, accessed April 21, 2016, http://scienceblogs.com/cortex/2007/01/29/milton-friedman-and-the-ration/.

7   Paul Krugman, "Who Was Milton Friedman?" *New York Review of Books*, February 15, 2007, accessed April 21, 2016, http://www.nybooks.com/articles/2007/02/15/who-was-milton-friedman/.

MODULE 4
THE AUTHORS' CONTRIBUTION

KEY POINTS

- Tversky and Kahneman showed that human decision-making is biased in systematic ways.

- Their research paved the way for a new discipline: behavioral economics* (a field in which psychological insights into human behavior are used to shed light on decision-making).

- Previous theoretical work—such as the US psychologist* Herbert Simon's* idea of bounded rationality*—laid the groundwork for Tversky and Kahneman's empirical* methods ("empirical" here referring to evidence that can be verified by observation).

Authors' Aims

Amos Tversky and Daniel Kahneman's 1974 paper "Judgment under Uncertainty: Heuristics and Biases" was a summary of their work on bias* and decision-making. They believed that this general overview of bias and the shortcomings of human decision-making would be of interest to readers outside the discipline of psychology, so they chose to place it in the journal *Science*—a generalist scientific journal with a large readership from all disciplines.

The work presented was a collaborative effort. In 1971 and 1972, the authors had worked together at the Oregon Research Institute, where they engaged in a considerable amount of research on heuristics* (rules of thumb or mental shortcuts used to solve problems). After their return to Israel, Tversky and Kahneman decided to review what they had learned about decision-making. This process was methodical, even perfectionist; they chose every word with

66 We published the article in *Science* because we thought that the prevalence of systematic biases in intuitive assessments and predictions could possibly be of interest to scholars outside psychology. This interest, however, could not be taken for granted, as I learned in an encounter with a well-known American philosopher at a party in Jerusalem. [As] I began my story he turned away, saying, 'I am not really interested in the psychology of stupidity.' The *Science* article turned out to be a rarity: an empirical psychological article that (some) philosophers and (a few) economists could and did take seriously. 99

Daniel Kahneman, "Daniel Kahneman—Biographical," *Nobelprize.org*

care. Kahneman wrote later, "On our usual schedule of spending afternoons together, a day in which we advanced by a sentence or two was considered quite productive. Our enjoyment of the process gave us unlimited patience, and we wrote as if the precise choice of every word were a matter of great moment."[1]

Approach

Tverksy and Kahneman took a novel approach to their work, using experimental questions to study decision-making. That is, instead of tackling the problem from a theoretical angle, they created experimental questions and puzzles for people to solve. They looked at the errors people made in doing so, and grouped these errors into categories. Analyzing the responses helped them to identify the general rules people seemed to be using as they solved the puzzles. Through this process Tversky and Kahneman identified some of the systematic heuristics (rules of thumb) that people were using.

Kahneman had adopted this approach to research as early as the late 1950s, when he was teaching in California at Berkeley. Writing about that time he says, "I was trying to develop a research program to study … motivation in children, using an approach that I called a 'psychology of single questions.' My model for this kind of psychology was research reported by [the US psychologist] Walter Mischel* in which he devised two questions that he posed to samples of children in Caribbean islands: 'You can have this (small) lollipop today, or this (large) lollipop tomorrow,' and 'Now let's pretend that there is a magic man … who could change you into anything that you would want to be, what you would want to be?' The responses to these lovely questions turned out to be plausibly correlated with numerous characteristics of the child and the child's background. I found this inspiring: Mischel had succeeded in creating a link between an important psychological concept and a simple operation to measure it. There was (and still is) almost nothing like it in psychology, where concepts are commonly associated with procedures that can be described only by long lists or by convoluted paragraphs of prose."[2]

Contribution in Context

Tversky and Kahneman are often credited with the invention of the field of behavioral economics. But their work did build on previous research. Even early economists such as the Scottish thinker Adam Smith* were aware of the many psychological subtleties involved in human decision-making. Smith wrote in 1759, "How selfish soever man may be supposed, there are evidently some principles in his nature, which interest him in the fortune of others, and render their happiness necessary to him, though he derives nothing from it except the pleasure of seeing it."[3] This comment is at odds with the fully rational man posited later by neoclassical* economists. In the nineteenth century, such economists attempted to cut all their ties with psychology and built an artificial "homo economicus"* (economic man), who is driven by self-interest and who always seeks to derive maximum benefit from his choices.

A century later, psychology returned to economics; in 1951 the Hungarian American psychologist George Katona* published the paper "Psychological Analysis of Economic Behavior,"[4] the foundation of the discipline of behavioral economics, which led to the creation of the *Journal of Behavioral Economics* in 1971. The term "behavioral economics" itself appeared for the first time in 1958,[5] and the term "heuristics" had been coined a year earlier by the American economist Herbert Simon.* As a result, academics in many disciplines were already aware of the ideas; the scholarly context was, therefore, very welcoming to Tversky and Kahneman's innovations, and the reason that their work made such an impact was because they succeeded in bringing behavioral economics to the attention of economists. According to some experts, their publications "altered the intellectual history of economics; they brought the behavioral economics research program into the mainstream."[6]

NOTES

1   Daniel Kahneman, "Experiences of Collaborative Research," *American Psychologist* 58, no. 9 (2003): 723–30.

2   Daniel Kahneman, "Daniel Kahneman—Biographical," Nobelprize.org, accessed April 21, 2016, http://www.nobelprize.org/nobel_prizes/economic-sciences/laureates/2002/kahneman-bio.html.

3   Adam Smith, *The Theory of Moral Sentiments*, Library of Economics and Liberty, accessed April 21, 2016, http://www.econlib.org/library/Smith/smMS1.html.

4   George Katona, *Psychological Analysis of Economic Behavior* (New York: McGraw-Hill, 1951).

5   David Laibson and Richard Zeckhauser, "Amos Tversky and the Ascent of Behavioral Economics," *Journal of Risk and Uncertainty* 16, no. 1 (1998): 7–47.

6   Laibson and Zeckhauser, "Amos Tversky," 19.

SECTION 2
IDEAS

MAIN IDEAS

KEY POINTS

- Tversky and Kahneman show that when we make decisions under conditions of uncertainty (that is, with incomplete information), we use mental shortcuts that can lead to fast and correct decisions.

- They also show that these mental shortcuts may lead us to make systematic errors (bias).*

- Tversky and Kahneman's article is full of examples that allow readers to see the flaws in their own decision-making—a method of presentation that makes the article very powerful.

Key Themes

The central themes of Amos Tversky and Daniel Kahneman's 1974 article "Judgment under Uncertainty: Heuristics and Biases" are, as the title suggests, heuristics* and biases. Heuristics are cognitive* tricks that our minds use—automatic, simple ways to make decisions in complex contexts. They are essentially mental shortcuts or rules of thumb. Although heuristics might fail unpredictably, sometimes they fail in ways that are predictable. These predictable failures of heuristics are known as biases; they often predispose us toward making incorrect decisions.

The article explores decision-making in conditions where the information needed to make the decision is missing or incomplete. Decision-making under uncertainty can be illustrated using the example of vision. When we judge the distance of an object using just our eyes, the information we collect is incomplete. We need a distance-measuring device to give us the exact measurement. So when we guess how far away an object is, we are operating under a condition of

❝ This article shows that people rely on a limited number of heuristic principles which reduce the complex tasks of assessing probabilities and predicting values to simpler judgmental operations. **❞**

Amos Tversky and Daniel Kahneman, "Judgment under Uncertainty: Heuristics and Biases"

uncertainty. To solve this, we tend to use cognitive tricks. For example, we use the size of an object as a clue. The further it is from us, the smaller it appears; as it moves closer or we move closer to it, it grows larger in our field of vision. This means we are using size as a *heuristic* to judge the distance. However, like most heuristics, its validity is limited to specific settings. In some situations, this heuristic (like others) can give rise to visual illusions.

We can predict the errors that heuristics create. As the output of a heuristic is always predictable, so are the errors resulting from it. In terms of the heuristic of size and distance, it is predictable that when we are presented with a big object, we will judge it to be closer to us than a small one—we will never assume the reverse. This is called a bias.

Exploring the Ideas

The three heuristics presented in the paper are *representativeness*, *availability*, and *adjustment and anchoring*.

To understand the heuristic of *representativeness*, consider that we judge things and people based on how representative of, or similar they are to, stereotypes. We do this while ignoring other information. For example: Steve is "shy, meek, and has very little interest in people." When asked, people might guess that Steve is a librarian, because the description resembles the stereotype of a librarian. So, while the stereotype might be informative, it may also lead us to the wrong conclusion.

Availability concerns the way in which people judge how often an event occurs based on how readily they can remember a similar event. To demonstrate this, Tversky and Kahneman devised a memory test. Participants were read a list of names, half female and half male. The lists contained the names of either very famous men or very famous women (but not both). When asked how many men/women had been listed, participants answered that there were more of the gender with the famous names. Their celebrity status made them more memorable. So while memory can help us make correct judgments, it can also distort those judgments, leading us to make errors.

Adjustment and anchoring concerns numbers. We tend to overweight the first numbers we see; this is "anchoring." Then, when we gain subsequent information, the adjustments we make tend to be insufficient. One group of people was asked to estimate the total for 8x7x6x5x4x3x2x1; another was asked to estimate the total for 1x2x3x4x5x6x7x8. The answer to both sums is the same—but the first group's estimation was higher than that of the second group; why? Because we give most weight to the first numbers we see; 8x7 is greater than 1x2.

As these examples show, heuristics can lead to bias. These biases often result in failures to solve problems effectively.

Language and Expression

While Tversky and Kahneman's "Judgment under Uncertainty" appeared in a scientific journal, it is not filled with highly technical jargon. In general the writing is clear, concise, and reasonably accessible. That said, the authors do assume that the reader has at least a working knowledge of concepts related to probability.

Tversky and Kahneman do a masterful job of providing specific, concrete examples of the points they are trying to make. These examples tend to engage readers and allow them to think about what their answer would have been. When the correct answer is described, they see for themselves how their own judgment is biased in systematic ways. Such personal demonstrations make Tversky and Kahneman's points in a salient, simple, and powerful way.

What was innovative about their work was that it drew a connection between heuristics and biases:

* A heuristic is a rule of thumb used as such in different contexts.
* A cognitive bias is a systematic error in our thinking.

This link between the two concepts did cause some problems. The term "bias" has a negative connotation when used in everyday language. As Kahneman says, "There is no denying, however, that the name of our method and approach created a strong association between heuristics and biases, and thereby contributed to giving heuristics a bad name, which we did not intend. I recently came to realize that the association of heuristics and biases has affected me as well."[1]

NOTES

1   Daniel Kahneman, "Daniel Kahneman—Biographical," Nobelprize.org, accessed April 21, 2016, http://www.nobelprize.org/nobel_prizes/economic-sciences/laureates/2002/kahneman-bio.html.

MODULE 6
SECONDARY IDEAS

KEY POINTS

- Biases* associated with heuristics* often result in relevant information being ignored or misused in reaching decisions.

- Researchers trained in statistics are influenced by their biases as much as anyone else; the tendency, then, is ingrained in the human mind.

- These biases affect the day-to-day decisions of both laypeople and experts—having a possible negative impact on scientific research.

Other Ideas

Amos Tversky and Daniel Kahneman's article "Judgment under Uncertainty: Heuristics and Biases" contains a number of secondary themes, each of which offers additional insight into the nature of the biases that result from the use of heuristics.

Sometimes people make biased decisions because they are motivated to do so. For instance, according to the bias of "wishful thinking," people form beliefs that please them, regardless of evidence to the contrary. But Tversky and Kahneman also demonstrate that we make errors of judgment even when we are motivated *not* to do so. They found that such errors were made even when participants were financially rewarded for giving the correct answer. Arguably this shows just how deep-rooted, automatic, and unconscious our cognitive biases must be.

Aside from the unconscious and automatic nature of these biases, there are a number of common assumptions and cognitive* biases that people seem to hold. One example is that individuals tend to disregard sample size when estimating probability. We seem to expect limited

❝ These biases are not attributable to motivational effects such as wishful thinking or the distortion of judgment by payoffs and penalties. Indeed, several of the severe errors of judgment reported earlier occurred despite the fact that subjects were encouraged to be accurate and were rewarded for the correct answer. The reliance on heuristics and the prevalence of biases are not restricted to laymen. Experienced researchers are also prone to the same biases—when they think intuitively. **❞**

Amos Tversky and Daniel Kahneman, "Judgment under Uncertainty: Heuristics and Biases"

sequences of events to reflect characteristics of all such events. We also make predictions based on intuition, are confident in decisions that are consistent with stereotypes, and ignore the fact that some variation across observations is to be expected.[1]

Exploring the Ideas

Why is it that we disregard sample size when estimating probability? This heuristic causes problems because the larger a sample, the more representative it is likely to be of the population from which it was drawn. Smaller samples are more likely to show deviations from the norm. Tversky and Kahneman comment that "this fundamental notion of statistics is evidently not part of people's repertoire of intuitions."[2]

Tversky and Kahneman point out that people also erroneously "expect that a sequence of events generated by random process will represent the essential characteristics of that process even when that sequence is short."[3] To illustrate this point, they point to an example involving coin tosses. People "regard the sequence H-T-H-T-T-H to be more likely than the sequence H-H-H-T-T-T, which does not appear random, and also more likely than the sequence H-H-H-H-T-H, which does not represent the fairness of the coin."[4] In other words, people seem to expect small sequences of events to reflect the overall pattern of those events. Furthermore, they tend to be perfectly willing to make predictions about some future outcome based on intuition and limited information—predicting, for example, that a company will be profitable in the future when given a positive description of that company, even if the description contains no information about profits.[5]

When people predict an outcome (whether or not a quiet man with thick glasses called Steve is a librarian, for example) they use the representativeness of the input—in this case, the description of Steve. Their confidence in their judgment depends on the degree of representativeness (here, the similarity between Steve and the stereotype of a librarian). This unwarranted confidence is common among psychologists* when conducting selection interviews: if the interviewee "looks like" a good candidate then the psychologist will recommend selecting that person.[6]

Overlooked

When "Judgment under Uncertainty" was first published, many people misunderstood what Tversky and Kahneman were saying. "The conclusions that readers drew were often too strong," Kahneman wrote. "Whereas we had shown that (some, not all) judgments about uncertain events are mediated by heuristics, which (sometimes, not always) produce predictable biases, we were often read as having claimed that people cannot think straight."[7]

This strong reaction to the Tversky and Kahneman paper can be explained by the fact that at the time, there was no global theory. The two researchers put together the "dual model" of thinking, according to which humans can make decisions in two ways—a fast, intuitive way, prone to systematic biases and errors, and another reflective, slower way that is less influenced by mental shortcuts and systematic errors. The subtle way in which Tversky and Kahneman's ideas can help to explain human reasoning and human behavior has often been overlooked. Kahneman concluded, almost 30 years later, that most of the controversy revolving around heuristics and biases could be resolved by applying the principles of the dual thinking model.[8]

Another reason for this original paper being misunderstood was that our automatic way of thinking is by definition not conscious. Therefore, it is difficult to believe that it has such a strong effect on our decisions. Our slower, reflective thought, on the other hand, is conscious, deliberate, and we are aware of it. When Tversky and Kahneman published their paper, researchers had little interest in conditions in which the deliberate mode of thinking is overridden.

So, the paper was initially misunderstood and created controversy; but ironically, this increased its impact in subsequent years.[9]

NOTES

1   Amos Tversky and Daniel Kahneman, "Judgment under Uncertainty: Heuristics and Biases," *Science* 185, no. 4157 (1974): 1124–31.

2   Tversky and Kahneman, "Judgment under Uncertainty," 1125.

3   Tversky and Kahneman, "Judgment under Uncertainty," 1125.

4   Tversky and Kahneman, "Judgment under Uncertainty," 1125.

5   Tversky and Kahneman, "Judgment under Uncertainty," 1126.

6   Tversky and Kahneman, "Judgment under Uncertainty," 1126.

7   Daniel Kahneman. "Daniel Kahneman—Biographical," Nobelprize.org, accessed April 21, 2016, http://www.nobelprize.org/nobel_prizes/economic-sciences/laureates/2002/kahneman-bio.html.

8   Daniel Kahneman and Shane Frederick, "Representativeness Revisited: Attribute Substitution in Intuitive Judgment," in *Heuristics and Biases: The Psychology of Intuitive Judgment*, ed. Thomas Gilovich, et al. (Cambridge: Cambridge University Press, 2002), 49–81.

MODULE 7
ACHIEVEMENT

KEY POINTS

- Tversky and Kahneman reached a large audience and had a bigger-than-expected impact (creating the field of behavioral economics* and leading to Kahneman's 2002 Nobel Prize).

- Their work had this impact because they were challenging such a popular model—the rational agent model.*

- When they published, they had not finalized their general theory; this led to some degree of misunderstanding and to harsh criticisms.

Assessing the Argument

When Amos Tversky and Daniel Kahneman published "Judgment under Uncertainty: Heuristics and Biases" in 1974, they placed the article in *Science*, a widely read scientific journal published by the American Association for the Advancement of Science. They were surprised by its impact. The article transformed the fields of psychology,* economics, and the social sciences;* philosophers, economists, and researchers adopted their techniques. "Judgment under Uncertainty" has been cited over 36,000 times—a considerable number for a psychology paper.[1]

Kahneman wrote later, "Our article attracted much more attention than we had expected, and it remains one of the most highly cited works in social science (more than three hundred scholarly articles referred to it in 2010). Scholars in other disciplines found it useful, and the ideas of heuristics* and biases* have been used productively in many fields."[2]

While the paper was intended to be a critique of the rational agent model, it was at first misinterpreted as a critique of human *rationality*.

❝ The main conclusion is that the huge impact of
Kahneman and Tversky's work is not due to the
accrual of confirmatory evidence, but, ironically, to its
imperfectness and the persistent failure to clearly define
and thus perhaps to falsify and discard the original
heuristics. **❞**

Klaus Fiedler and Momme von Sydow, "Heuristics and Biases: Beyond
Tversky and Kahneman's Judgment under Uncertainty," *Cognitive
Psychology: Revisiting the Classic Studies*

Some readers thought the main point was that "humans are dumb."
Kahneman wrote in his Nobel Price lecture that certain readers had
arrived at conclusions that were false: "We were often read as having
claimed that people cannot think straight."[3]

Kahneman wrote later that he and Tversky did not deliberately try
to reach such a large audience: "I realized only recently how fortunate
we were not to have aimed deliberately at the large target we happened
to hit. If we had intended the article as a challenge to the rational
model, we would have written it differently, and the challenge would
have been less effective."[4]

Achievement in Context
The paper's popularity and impact can be attributed to the quality of
the research and the academic climate at the time of its publication.
For many decades, research on decision-making had remained in the
shadow of the neoclassical model* of rational agent theory:* we act
rationally, the model says, with perfect understanding of the various
advantages and disadvantages our actions might bring.

Scholars knew the model was not satisfactory, and had already
started searching for alternatives. In the 1950s and 1960s, economists
such as Herbert Simon* and psychologists such as George Katona*

had introduced the concepts of bounded rationality* (the idea that perfectly rational behavior is limited by available information) and heuristics, and had tried to reconcile psychology and economics. The foundation of modern behavioral economics* can be traced back to those years. The conditions were therefore ripe for Tversky and Kahneman's heuristics and biases research program.

While economics and psychology were becoming reacquainted, psychology itself was transforming. Since the 1950s, behaviorism* had dominated the field. Behaviorists were not interested in our internal mental states—our emotions or cognition;* they were only interested in the outward behavior that they could observe. However, the dominance of behaviorism was about to crumble. In the 1950s, several disciplines joined together to redefine psychological research. This resulted in cognitive science becoming a discipline in and of itself. Psychologists could now explore hidden mental processes, using methods and models from other fields such as computer science, philosophy, and neuroscience* (the study of the physical constitution of the brain and nervous system).

The American psychologist Herbert Simon was one of the first researchers to compare the human brain to a computer, introducing concepts of rules and heuristics. So when Tversky and Kahneman published their articles, the set of analogies and metaphors comparing the brain to a computer had already penetrated the field of psychology. This helped to prepare the way for their ideas.

Limitations

Tversky and Kahneman's influence went far beyond economics and psychology. Their work was read in many countries and is still influential today. While its reach can be credited in part to the popularity of the rational agent model that it criticized, it also created its own sphere of influence.

In 2002 the political scientist Jack S. Levy* indicated the degree to which Tversky and Kahneman had influenced the social sciences: "The rise of the behavioral economics research program owes a great deal to psychologists Daniel Kahneman and Amos Tversky, whose research on systematic deviations from rationality quickly transcended their own discipline and significantly influenced other fields, including management science, finance, investment, and consumer economics. Their work has recently begun to influence political psychology, international relations, and other areas of political science."[5]

Political scientists had long known that the rational agent model was not answering all their needs. The American economist Anthony Downs* had published his book *An Economic Theory of Democracy* in 1957, which showed that strictly applying the rational agent model to voting behavior predicts a much lower voter turnout—0 percent—than what is actually observed. So although this model allowed scholars to study voting behavior in a controlled way, political science also needed a more realistic model for decision-making.[6] After Tversky and Kahneman published their work, political scientists drew on their ideas to address the limitations of the rational agent model.

Tversky and Kahneman's influence can also be found in the field of business. As an example, the business scholars Max Bazerman* and Don A. Moore's* influential textbook *Judgment in Managerial Decision Making* (2012) devotes a good third of its content to work conducted or inspired by Tversky and Kahneman's heuristics and biases research program.[7]

NOTES

1   Google Scholar, "Judgment under Uncertainty," accessed April
    21, 2016, https://scholar.google.com/citations?view_op=view_
    citation&hl=en&user=9puL9pAAAAAJ&citation_for_view=9puL9pAAAAAJ:u-
    x6o8ySGOsC.

2   Daniel Kahneman, *Thinking, Fast and Slow* (New York: Farrar, Straus and
    Giroux, 2011), 8.

3   Daniel Kahneman, "Daniel Kahneman—Biographical," Nobelprize.org,
    accessed April 21, 2016, http://www.nobelprize.org/nobel_prizes/economic-
    sciences/laureates/2002/kahneman-bio.html.

4   Kahneman, "Daniel Kahneman—Biographical."

5   Jack S. Levy, "Daniel Kahneman: Judgment, Decision, and Rationality,"
    Political Science & Politics 35, no. 2 (2002): 271–3.

6   Anthony Downs, *An Economic Theory of Democracy* (New York: Harper &
    Row, 1957).

7   Max Bazerman and Don A. Moore, *Judgment in Managerial Decision
    Making*, 8th edn (New York: Wiley, 2013).

PLACE IN THE AUTHORS' WORK

KEY POINTS

- Kahneman's work revolves around human judgment and decision-making; Tversky was studying measurement* and expected utility theory.*

- Together they developed three lines of research: the study of heuristics* and biases* in decision-making; prospect theory,* describing the way humans make choices under conditions of uncertainty; and the study of the dual system of decision-making.

- Kahneman received the Nobel Prize in 2002 for his work on heuristics and biases; by this time, Tversky had already died.

Positioning

Daniel Kahneman and Amos Tversky's 1974 article "Judgment under Uncertainty: Heuristics and Biases" was published early in both authors' careers. It was one of their first collaborative works and kick-started a long and fruitful collaboration.

This collaboration followed three broad phases. First, they conducted a series of ingenious experiments that revealed some human heuristics and their associated biases. This research gave birth to the heuristic-and-bias research program that is still influential today. It was during this phase of their work together that "Judgment under Uncertainty" was published.

In their second phase, Tversky and Kahneman investigated how human decision-making deviates from the predictions generated by the rational agent model.* The set of rules and deviations they discovered was formalized under the name of "prospect theory," which attempted to explain how humans make decisions under conditions of uncertainty.

66 In the 1960s, Kahneman is predominantly working on the psychophysics of vision ... During the 1960s, Tversky for his part works predominantly on the theoretical exploration and development of EUT (Expected Utility Theory) ... The different lines of research of Kahneman and Tversky come together in their collaborative work of the 1970s. 99

Floris Heukelom, "Kahneman and Tversky and the Origin of Behavioral Economics"

In the last phase of their collaboration, Tversky and Kahneman worked on reconciling the two modes of human decision-making: the thoughtful, rational approach that we are consciously aware of, and our subconscious,* faster, intuition-driven approach.

Their collaboration came to an end with Tversky's death in 1996, when he was just 59. His contributions to the social sciences had been monumental. When he met Kahneman, he had already exerted a major impact on ideas about decision-making across numerous disciplines, including psychology,* statistics, law, medicine, and business.[1] Tversky published 124 papers over his career; some of his most cited and influential papers were among the 24 he published with Kahneman.[2]

Integration

Prior to starting an academic career, Kahneman's early work had focused on judgment and decision-making in real-world settings. During his years in the Israeli army he designed assessments and selection tools, and had gained his first insights into the biased nature of human decision-making. At the time, however, he lacked the theoretical background to put these observations into perspective. When Kahneman came to the United States in the 1960s, his research focused on visual perception and visual judgment.

Tversky's work in the 1960s, on the other hand, was mostly concerned with the theoretical development of expected utility theory* as a normative* theory.[3] "Normative" refers to what people *should* do according to their beliefs and values, while "descriptive"* refers to what they *actually* do.

Kahneman and Tversky's different lines of research came together in their collaboration of the 1970s. Tversky's work on normative theory and the measurement of actual choice complemented Kahneman's work on the difference between the objective stimulus (the external circumstances provoking the decision) and subjective sensation (the personal, internal mental state informing the decision). Together they could apply their empirical* work on decision-making to real-world situations. Their work on prospect theory, a theoretical framework for studying decision-making, was set out in "Choices, Values, and Frames" (1984);[4] their attempt to reconcile the two modes of human decision-making (one rational, slow, and conscious; the other intuitive, fast, and automatic) was addressed in Kahneman's book *Thinking, Fast and Slow* (2011).[5]

Significance

Tversky and Kahneman received much positive attention for "Judgment under Uncertainty," and soon emerged as the leading scholars on decision-making. However, it was the publication of their framework for analyzing decisions, "Prospect Theory" (1979), that propelled them to fame. "Prospect Theory," which has been cited nearly 40,000 times,[6] helped Kahneman earn the Nobel Prize. However, had their 1974 paper not been so widely read, it is hard to say whether their later work would have been so influential. Certainly, these two publications formed the cornerstone of Tversky and Kahneman's careers. It is also true that "Prospect Theory" grew out of their earlier work. In this paper, the two argue that rather than decisions being based solely on final outcomes, they are affected by what individuals perceive they may lose or gain. It takes into account issues such as our attitudes to risk, which are ignored by the expected utility model* of economics.

The most important phase of both Tversky and Kahneman's careers was when they collaborated together. The American economists David Laibson* and Richard Zeckhauser* conducted an analysis of Tversky's intellectual influence and concluded that there was a "remarkable synergy between Tversky and Kahneman" and that of the top 20 papers that had the "greatest impact throughout the social sciences—14 represent Tversky and Kahneman collaborations."[7]

NOTES

1   Daniel Kahneman, "Daniel Kahneman—Biographical," Nobelprize.org, accessed April 21, 2016, http://www.nobelprize.org/nobel_prizes/economic-sciences/laureates/2002/kahneman-bio.html.

2   David Laibson and Richard Zeckhauser, "Amos Tversky and the Ascent of Behavioral Economics," *Journal of Risk and Uncertainty*, 16, no. 1 (1998): 7–47; and Amos Tversky and Daniel Kahneman. "Judgment under Uncertainty: Heuristics and Biases," *Science* 185, no. 4157 (1974): 1124–31.

3   Floris Heukelom, "Kahneman and Tversky and the Origin of Behavioral Economics," Tinbergen Institute Discussion Paper TI 2007–003/1 (2007): 1.

4   Daniel Kahneman and Amos Tversky, "Choices, Values, and Frames," *American Psychologist* 39, no. 4 (1984): 341–50.

5   Daniel Kahneman, *Thinking, Fast and Slow* (New York: Farrar, Strauss and Giroux, 2011).

6   Google Scholar, "Prospect Theory," accessed April 21, 2016, https://scholar.google.com/scholar?hl=en&q=prospect+theory&btnG=&as_sdt=1%2C9&as_sdtp=.

7   Laibson and Zeckhauser, "Amos Tversky," 17.

SECTION 3
IMPACT

MODULE 9
THE FIRST RESPONSES

KEY POINTS

- The initial reception of "Judgment under Uncertainty" was almost exclusively positive—once its readers understood that Tversky and Kahneman were *not* saying that humans are inherently stupid.

- Over time, however, and after the publication of "Prospect Theory" in 1979, criticism began to emerge.

- Kahneman and Tversky adopted the policy of not criticizing their critics.

Criticism

The initial conclusion many readers drew about Amos Tversky and Daniel Kahneman's "Judgment under Uncertainty: Heuristics and Biases" was that it was an attack on human rationality ("humans are dumb") rather than an attack on the rational agent model* as the authors had intended.[1] Once this misunderstanding was cleared up, the book received a mostly positive reception until about 1990— albeit with exceptions.

The American psychologist* Jonathan Cohen* claimed that the mathematical model used by Tversky and Kahneman to highlight the representativeness heuristic* was wrong (this is the heuristic in which a person judges the nature or identity of other people and things by comparing them to stereotypes).[2]

Economists like Hillel Einhorn* and Robin Hogarth* questioned the normative* foundation for Tversky and Kahneman's work on decision-making. Developing normative decision-making models implies that researchers can compute the "right" answer to a given

> **❝** Whatever the reason, the article soon became a standard reference as an attack on the rational-agent model, and it spawned a large literature in cognitive science, philosophy, and psychology. We had not anticipated that outcome. **❞**
>
> Daniel Kahneman, "Daniel Kahneman—Biographical," *Nobelprize.org*

problem. This lies at the core of Tversky and Kahneman's paper: they describe a series of problems, and compare participants' responses to the "correct" ones. Einhorn and Hogarth felt that there was no unequivocal norm with which human decision-making could be compared. In their article "Behavioral Decision Theory" (1981),[3] they argue that if atoms failed to follow the laws supposed to describe their behavior, we would not label that behavior "irrational." Instead, we would question the validity of the laws we had created. "Why then, should we do so with Human decision-making?"[4] The authors point out that since the normative model is only a model, it can be wrong.[5]

The criticism rumbles on. The normative model also relies on many assumptions that may not always be correct. This was addressed by the German psychologist Klaus Fiedler* in 2015, who wrote, "Allegedly irrational judgments and decisions can often be re-interpreted in terms of reasonable assumptions about the task and the problem setting."[6]

Responses

Tversky and Kahneman replied to a few specific criticisms—for instance to Cohen's 1979 article in which he claimed that the mathematical model they had used to highlight the representativeness heuristic was wrong, and that their normative model should use a different model of probability.[7] They claimed that Cohen's proposed model was inadequate and that the data still supported the existence of the heuristic.[8]

After replying to a few critics, they decided that further comment was pointless, because of the misconceptions about their intent in publishing the article. Indeed, Kahneman claims that "After participating in a few published skirmishes in the early 80s, Amos and I adopted a policy of not criticizing the critiques of our work."[9] However, they felt compelled to make an exception in 1996 to address specific points voiced by their most fierce critic, the German psychologist Gerd Gigerenzer.*[10]

Instead of replying to specific criticisms, Kahneman and Tversky carried on with their work; the next notable development after "Judgment under Uncertainty: Heuristics and Biases" was "Prospect Theory," published in 1979.[11] This was important because it established a formal framework for what had been, so far, mostly empirical* work—work founded on observable evidence. This resolved some, if not all, of the issues raised by the academic community.

Conflict And Consensus

"Judgment under Uncertainty" had a tremendous impact, not only on psychology and economics but also on the social sciences* in general. The powerful demonstrations it offered profoundly changed the way practitioners in many fields (notably economics, finance, and management) approached decision-making. It is now common to think and talk about decision-making without making the assumption that all decisions are made rationally. The criticisms did not affect the paper's wider sphere of influence, although they were felt in the subfield of psychology concerned with judgment and decision-making.

The impact and influence of Tversky and Kahneman's work may be due to the fact that they continued to develop it. They started by building a theoretical framework, prospect theory,* which explained some of the heuristics and biases* they had identified. Later, they broadened their research via the dual system theory (the idea that humans make decisions in two ways: one conscious, one automatic). These additions to their model made their heuristics and biases research program even more comprehensible and useful for practitioners of all fields.

These extensions did not resolve the initial criticisms of their theory—rather, they raised additional critiques and questions. But they did help the theory become known even more widely and increased its influence.

While there is still much support for Tversky and Kahneman's work globally, the critics remain fierce. To this day, the German psychologist Gerd Gigerenzer remains a very strong opponent. He argues that heuristics need not be thought of as shortcuts that result in reduced accuracy. Rather he conceives of a "toolbox" of heuristics available for specific circumstances.[12]

NOTES

1   Daniel Kahneman, "Daniel Kahneman—Biographical," Nobelprize.org, accessed April 21, 2016, http://www.nobelprize.org/nobel_prizes/economic-sciences/laureates/2002/kahneman-bio.html.

2   Jonathan L. Cohen, "On the Psychology of Prediction: Whose is the Fallacy?" *Cognition* 7, no. 4 (1979): 385–407.

3   Hillel J. Einhorn and Robin M. Hogarth, "Behavioral Decision Theory: Processes of Judgment and Choice," *Journal of Accounting Research* 19, no. 1 (1981): 1–31.

4   Einhorn and Hogarth, "Behavioral Decision Theory," 1–31.

5   Einhorn and Hogarth, "Behavioral Decision Theory," 1–31.

6   Klaus Fiedler and Momme von Sydow, "Heuristics and Biases: Beyond Tversky and Kahneman's (1974) Judgment under Uncertainty," in *Cognitive Psychology: Revisiting the Classical Studies*, ed. Michael W. Eysenck and David Groome (London: Sage Publishers, 2015), 150.

7   Cohen, "On the Psychology of Prediction."

8   Daniel Kahneman and Amos Tversky, "On the Interpretation of Intuitive Probability: A Reply to Jonathan Cohen," *Cognition* 7, no. 4 (1979): 409–11.

9   Kahneman, "Daniel Kahneman—Biographical."

10 Daniel Kahneman and Amos Tversky, "On the Reality of Cognitive Illusions," *Psychological Review* 103, no.3 (1996): 582–91.

11 Daniel Kahneman and Amos Tversky, "Prospect Theory: An Analysis of Decision Under Risk," *Econometrica: Journal of the Econometric Society* 47, no. 2 (1979): 263–91.

12 Gerd Gigerenzer, "The Adaptive Toolbox," in *Bounded Rationality: The Adaptive Toolbox*, ed. G. Gigerenzer and R. Selten (Cambridge, MA: MIT Press, 2001), 37–50.

MODULE 10
THE EVOLVING DEBATE

KEY POINTS

- "Judgment under Uncertainty" was key to the emergence of the new field of behavioral economics:* the science of using behavioral insights, psychology,* cognitive science* (the study of the ways in which we arrive at knowledge through thought), and neuroscience* (the study of the brain and nervous system) to understand and predict people's economic decisions.

- Other movements have emerged such as behavioral finance* (the study of human behavior and psychology in financial decision-making), and behavioral insights have been applied to governmental policy.

- The use of behavioral insights in public policy raises significant ethical and privacy concerns; they can be used for good purposes (nudging people into taking healthy choices, for instance) but could also be used as a powerful way to control populations.

Uses And Problems

Amos Tversky and Daniel Kahneman's 1974 paper "Judgment under Uncertainty: Heuristics and Biases" was widely adopted within the social sciences.* Its ideas shifted the focus in decision-making research from the study of rationality to the documentation of persistent biases.*

But the pair still have critics. In 1996 the German psychologist Gerd Gigerenzer* engaged the work's authors in a published debate.[1] After that, Kahneman stopped responding, because he felt that Gigerenzer was not "listening to their main argument."[2]

> ❝ For many years the predominant view in the social sciences had been that the rationality assumption is an adequate approximation for modeling and predicting human behavior ... But then, motivated by Simon's (1955) notions of bounded rationality and later by Kahneman and Tversky's heuristics and biases program ... the emphasis shifted toward documenting the persistent inadequacy of the rationality assumption. ❞
>
> Eldar Shafir and Robyn A. LeBoeuf, "Rationality,"
> *Annual Review of Psychology*

Gigerenzer's main point was that the norms used by Tversky and Kahneman to judge participants' responses were wrong and that, therefore, the "errors" they documented were actually errors of the model, not the participants. He claimed that when some of the biases documented were formulated differently, in terms of frequencies rather than probability, they disappeared. Tversky and Kahneman directly refuted this in response.[3]

Gigerenzer also claimed that the models of reasoning provided by Tversky and Kahneman were too vague. He called their heuristics* and biases "labels with the virtue of Rorschach inkblots:* a researcher can read into them what he or she wishes."[4] (Rorschach inkblots have been used by psychologists as a means of gaining insight into the subconscious* mind.)

Another German psychologist, Klaus Fiedler,* questioned Tversky and Kahneman's notion of anchoring:* the idea that when people make a numerical estimate they start with an initial number (an "anchor"). They adjust this as they gain new information, but— according to Tversky and Kahneman—this adjustment is insufficient, with the result that they arrive at a biased number. For Fiedler, however, "hardly any research has ever attempted to demonstrate a gradual process of insufficient adjustment of an initial anchor value.

[The fact that] anchoring effects may originate in a variety of different cognitive processes is tantamount to giving up the specific process suggested in the heuristic's original account."[5]

Schools Of Thought

Within psychology, Kahneman and Tversky's work offered a bridge between two movements: psychoanalysis* (a therapeutic and theoretical approach to the study of the subconscious mind) and cognitive psychology* (the study of the nature and processes of thought). Psychoanalysis is interested in subconscious processes and their influence on our behavior, while cognitive science is more interested in *measureable* cognitive mechanisms and processes. Tversky and Kahneman's work highlights the influence of unconscious processes on our behavior. In one example of the way their work has been used, the German psychologist Norbert Schwarz,* a researcher on human emotions, has demonstrated that people arrive at opinions using emotions as a heuristic.[6]

Two schools of thought emerged from the researchers' work. One embraced their ideas; most of the criticisms directed at the heuristics and biases program were dismissed over time, and a 2002 review lists more than 200 references that support it.[7]

The other school is headed by the German psychologist Gerd Gigerenzer. He has created an alternative approach to the study of decision-making—the fast and frugal heuristics program. Instead of studying specific biases or deviations from the norm, this program describes the cognitive model that is needed for people to perform well in a given environment. For Gigerenzer, heuristics, rather than being the product of cognitive limitations, represent a "bet." The person using the heuristic is making a bet about the structure of the surrounding environment. The metaphor guiding this program is that of an adaptive toolbox:* a simple decisions mechanism with each strategy tuned to a particular environment.[8]

In Current Scholarship

Tversky and Kahneman's work led to the new discipline of behavioral economics, which emerged in the 1980s. Before long, a large group of scholars began to conduct research premised on their work. American economists like Richard Thaler,* Colin Camerer,* David Laibson,* and the American legal scholar Cass Sunstein* all worked under the sponsorship of the Russell Sage Foundation,* an American foundation that sponsors research in social science and that sponsored a "Behavioral Economics Roundtable."[9] This research led to two approaches, distinguished by their methodology.*

The first uses the "descriptive" approach.* This attempts to describe how normal people actually make decisions. Researchers first try to analyze how people make decisions, then build models that predict the decision outcome and reflect the reality of the decision-making process. Researchers using the descriptive approach have also started a "prescriptive" movement. This is nudge theory,* which advocates using behavioral insights to help people make the "right" decisions.

The second is the "positive" approach. This is focused on determining if predictions made about people's behavior are mathematically correct. These researchers are interested in models that predict behavior *regardless of whether the model itself reflects the decision-making process*. Researchers from this perspective have taken valuable psychological insights and applied them to traditional economics.[10]

Besides researchers in academia, the work of many theorists and commentators relies on the trail blazed by Tversky and Kahneman. Notable texts include *Predictably Irrational* (2009) by the Israeli American psychologist Dan Ariely,* *Freakonomics* (2005) by the economist Steven Levitt* and the journalist Stephen Dubner,* and *Why Smart People Make Big Money Mistakes and How to Correct Them* (2010) by the American media consultant Gary Belsky* and the psychologist Thomas Gilovich.[11] These are just some of the popular science and self-help books that have arisen directly as a result of Tversky and Kahneman's work on judgments and decision-making, and the ensuing developments in the science of behavioral economics.

NOTES

1   Gerd Gigerenzer. "On Narrow Norms and Vague Heuristics: A Reply to Kahneman and Tversky," *Psychological Review* 103, no. 3 (1996): 592–6.

2   Daniel Kahneman, "Daniel Kahneman—Biographical," Nobelprize.org, accessed April 21, 2016, http://www.nobelprize.org/nobel_prizes/economic-sciences/laureates/2002/kahneman-bio.html.

3   Daniel Kahneman and Amos Tversky, "On the Reality of Cognitive Illusions," *Psychological Review* 103, no. 3 (1996): 582–91.

4   Gigerenzer. "On Narrow Norms."

5   Klaus Fiedler and Momme von Sydow, "Heuristics and Biases: Beyond Tversky and Kahneman's (1974) Judgment under Uncertainty," in *Cognitive Psychology: Revisiting the Classic Studies,* ed. Michael W. Eysenck and David Groome, 146–61 (London: Sage Publications, 2015).

6   Norbert Schwarz, "Emotion, Cognition, and Decision Making," *Cognition & Emotion* 14, no. 4 (2000): 433–40.

7   Eldar Shafir and Robyn A. LeBoeuf, "Rationality," *Annual Review of Psychology* 53, no. 1 (2002); 491–517.

8   A. Wilke and R. Mata, "Cognitive Bias," in *The Encyclopedia of Human Behavior*, vol. 1, ed. V. S. Ramachandran (New York: Academic Press, 2012), 531–5.

9   Russell Sage Foundation, Behavioral Economics Roundtable, accessed April 23, 2016, http://www.russellsage.org/research/behavioral-economics/behavioral-economics-roundtable.

10 Floris Heukelom, "Kahneman and Tversky and the Origin of Behavioral Economics," Tinbergen Institute Discussion Paper TI 2007–003/1 (2007): 1.

11 Dan Ariely, *Predictably Irrational: The Hidden Forces That Shape Our Decisions* (New York: HarperCollins, 2009); Steven D. Levitt and Stephen J. Dubner, *Freakonomics: A Rogue Economist Explores the Hidden Side of Everything* (New York: William Morrow, 2006); and Gary Belsky and Thomas Gilovich, *Why Smart People Make Big Money Mistakes and How to Correct Them: Lessons from the Life-Changing Science of Behavioral Economics* (New York: Simon & Schuster, 2010).

MODULE 11
IMPACT AND INFLUENCE TODAY

KEY POINTS

- "Judgment under Uncertainty" helped develop the field of behavioral science* and Kahneman and Tversky's heuristics* and biases* research has been hugely influential.

- Although the article successfully challenged the rational agent model* (the central tenet of neoclassical* economics), economists have yet to find a satisfying model that fully reflects their insights.

- The research on heuristics and biases has led to the development of many programs in public policy, economics, and finance.

Position

Amos Tversky and Daniel Kahneman's "Judgment under Uncertainty: Heuristics and Biases" has been widely adopted in academia and by practitioners of decision science—the scientific study of the decision-making process.[1] The ideas became mainstream, transforming popular discourse about the subject. This is reflected in the emergence of general audience books such as the best-selling *Freakonomics* (2005) by the economist Steven Levitt* and the journalist Stephen Dubner,* and *Nudge* (2008) by the American legal scholar Cass Sunstein* and the economist Richard Thaler.*[2]

The field of behavioral economics★ emerged from Tversky and Kahneman's work. Thinkers in this area such as Thaler and the psychologist* Dan Ariely* built a large part of their career on insights developed by the two. While classical economics had been dominated

❝ The impact of [Tversky and Kahneman's] research on the development of cognitive, social, and applied psychology was immense. Nowadays, textbooks and curricula in behavioral science are unimaginable without sizeable parts devoted to heuristics and biases **❞**

Klaus Fiedler and Momme von Sydow, "Heuristics and Biases: Beyond Tversky and Kahneman's Judgment under Uncertainty," *Cognitive Psychology: Revisiting the Classic Studies*

by the rational agent model, which claimed that people make economic decisions efficiently and rationally in their own self-interest, Tversky and Kahneman showed there were profound limits to human rationality.

As Kahneman and Tversky identified that humans do not take the decisions predicted by the rational agent model, they moved from a normative* decision-making model (what people *should* do) to a descriptive* one (what people *really* do). Their research contained another important insight: it suggested that even when people are told where they go wrong in their decision-making, they often cannot understand these reasons, and so cannot learn to make a better decision next time. While this is harmless in the case of abstract problems like the ones used by Tversky and Kahneman in their original paper, it can be a problem when it comes to real-life decisions (for example, when people say they would like to have money for their retirement but then are not able to save).

Interaction

Aspects of Tversky and Kahneman's work have been criticized by some psychologists who specialize in decision-making, but among the wider community of decision-making scientists, other scholars, and the public, their assumptions and theories have been widely adopted.

The general idea of using behavioral insights to understand how people make decisions—and subsequently being able to nudge them into taking a specific decision—is now used in many fields.

One of the leading proponents of using behavioral insights in finance is the American economist Richard Thaler, who has led a number of projects on the topic and has also started an investment company built around the tenets of behavioral finance.* In behavioral economics, one of the most recognized scientists is the Israeli American psychologist Dan Ariely,* whose work consolidated Kahneman and Tversky's legacy.

In public policy, the American legal scholar Cass Sunstein* and Thaler initiated a movement called "nudge"* or "light paternalism." This movement uses behavioral science and behavioral insights gained through experiments to design public policies. While they did not conduct all the research used in the concept's formulation, they wrote an important work explaining it, called *Nudge*. Published in 2008, the book draws on psychology and the behavioral sciences; notably, it suggests both that the state can decide what is best for people and that it can nudge them to adopt the behaviors that are best for them.[3]

The Continuing Debate

The ideas of prescriptive decision-making (that is, believing it is a good idea to help people think well and make better decisions) have not been debated in as much depth as might have been expected. Yet the concept of modifying products, policies, and messages based on behavioral insights is now relatively standard—or, at least, is on the way to becoming so. For instance, companies like Facebook and Google analyze their users' behaviors and generate income through targeted advertising based on these insights.

In addition, nudging and behavioral insights have been in the public sphere for at least a decade. In 2010 the United Kingdom became the first country to organize a nudge unit as part of the prime minister's office. Using behavioral economics and psychological insights into the behavior of taxpayers, the nudge unit was able to increase tax revenue by £200 million just by changing the wording of a letter sent to them. Since then, other countries have created nudge units that are linked tightly with the government: US president Barack Obama's* administration created one in 2015, as did Angela Merkel's* government in Germany.

There has been opposition to the idea that states should nudge their citizens into making better choices. The concept of nudge questions basic assumptions about freedom and democracy.[4] These voices have, so far, remained restricted to those of experts in the field, but they may become more influential as other nudge units are created across the globe.

NOTES

1   Daniel Kahneman and Amos Tversky, "Prospect Theory: An Analysis of Decision Under Risk," *Econometrica: Journal of the Econometric Society* 47, no. 2 (1979): 263–91.

2   Steven D. Levitt and Stephen J. Dubner, *Freakonomics: A Rogue Economist Explores the Hidden Side of Everything* (New York: William Morrow, 2006); Richard H. Thaler and Cass. R. Sunstein, *Nudge* (New Haven, CT: Yale University Press, 2008).

3   Thaler and Sunstein, *Nudge*.

4   Kitty S. Jones, "Cameron's Nudge that Knocked Democracy Down: Mind the Mindspace," *Politics and Insight*, December 17, 2014, accessed April 21, 2016, https://kittysjones.wordpress.com/2014/12/17/camerons-nudge-that-knocked-democracy-down-mind-the-mindspace/.

MODULE 12
WHERE NEXT?

KEY POINTS

- "Judgment under Uncertainty" opened the way for the emergence of a popular new field: behavioral economics.*

- Behavioral insights are now being used to nudge people to make the "right" decision

- The article revolutionized psychology* and economics, offering a viable alternative to the then-dominant model of decision-making: the rational agent model.

Potential

Amos Tversky and Daniel Kahneman's "Judgment under Uncertainty: Heuristics and Biases" challenged the dominant model of neoclassical economics,* which assumed that decision-making is essentially rational, and laid the foundation for the emergence of a new field of study: behavioral economics. This new field is now growing rapidly and attracting ever more researchers and practitioners.

We live in a world where hyper-segmentation of groups and customers and hyper-customization of products and messaging is made possible by the advancement of technology. The "big data" trend is a reflection of this (that is, the trend toward gathering very large sets of data that can be analyzed using computers to reveal information about everything from weather patterns to how people behave). Behavioral economics and its close relative, behavioral insights, are benefiting from this new trend; it therefore seems probable that an increasing number of people and businesses will make use of their approaches. As a result, Tversky and Kahneman's text is likely to remain important.

❝The past decade has been a triumph for behavioral economics, the fashionable cross-breed of psychology and economics. Behavioral economics is one of the hottest ideas in public policy.❞

Daniel Kahneman, "Behavioural Economics and Public Policy," *Financial Times*

Besides behavioral insights, another theory that has grown out of their work is that of "nudge,"* which relates to the management of behavior, and promises to deliver more efficient public policies at a lower cost. Since government debt is growing, the influence of nudging on public policy is also sure to grow in the future. As the *Economist* points out, "'Freakonomics' was the book that made the public believe the dismal science has something interesting to say about how people act in the real world, although it was 'Nudge' was the one that got policy wonks excited. The book, first published in 2008, is about the potential for behavioral economics to improve the effectiveness of government."[1] This trend, too, will help to maintain the status of "Judgment under Uncertainty" as a deeply influential text.

Future Directions

The group of scholars involved in the roundtable convened by the Russell Sage Foundation,*[2] a foundation that sponsors research in social science, is continuing to research and evangelize about the benefits of using behavioral insights and behavioral economics to influence behavior. Many of these scholars, including the American economists Richard Thaler,* Colin Camerer,* David Laibson,* George Loewenstein,* and the legal scholar Cass Sunstein,* are engaged in academic work related to decision-making. Some of them also conduct practical research. This research is then used by their clients (businesses and governments) to ensure the long-term influence of the behavioral economics approach.

An example of a successful application of the behavioral economics approach is the "save more tomorrow" program,[3] designed to solve the retirement savings problem in the United States. When asked, most people would like to save more for retirement and to be sure they will have enough money when the time comes for them to stop working. Although, most people actually fail at saving money because of an overvaluation of their present needs. The solution offered by the "save more tomorrow" program is to ask employees if they would like to save the extra money they will get following their next raise. This program led to a 68 percent increase in pension enrollment and an increase in savings by about 7 percent.[4]

Summary

"Judgment under Uncertainty" is essential reading for anyone interested in decision-making. The article demonstrates that our decision-making processes are driven, at a subconscious* level, by our cognitive* heuristics* and biases.* While these heuristics often lead us to the right decision, they may also lead our decisions astray.

Tversky and Kahneman's article has been cited almost 36,000 times, an astounding record for a psychology publication.[5] This, and subsequent research by the authors, won Kahneman a Nobel Prize in Economic Sciences in 2002, the very first awarded to a psychologist, which Tversky surely would have shared had he not died in 1996.

When people make decisions, they *feel* they make them consciously, and most of the time for good reasons. This seminal paper shows that this is not always true. In fact, most of our decisions are made subconsciously and are biased by our emotions, intuitions, and our cognitive constraints and limitations.

Tversky and Kahneman's work realized two impressive goals at once. It challenged the assumption of neoclassical economics that all economic agents are rational—that they have all the information, and always take the choice that maximizes the benefit to them. Simultaneously, it sparked the creation of a new field: behavioral economics—a science that uses behavioral insights to describe and nudge people towards taking the "right" direction. Although this raises problems with regard to freedom, democracy, and privacy, the trend has been growing.

Both these achievements ensure that Tversky and Kahneman's work will remain relevant for a long time to come.

NOTES

1   *Economist*, "Nudge Nudge, Think Think: The Use of Behavioral Economics in Public Policy Shows Promise," March 24, 2012, accessed April 21, 2016, http://www.economist.com/node/21551032.

2   Russell Sage Foundation, Behavioral Economics Roundtable, accessed April 23, 2016, http://www.russellsage.org/research/behavioral-economics/behavioral-economics-roundtable.

3   Richard H. Thaler and Shlomo Benartzi, "Save More Tomorrow: Using Behavioral Economics to Increase Employee Saving," *Journal of Political Economy* 112, no. 1 (2004): S164–S187.

4   Justin Fox, "From 'Economic Man' to Behavioral Economics," *Harvard Business Review*, May 2015, accessed April 21, 2016, https://hbr.org/2015/05/from-economic-man-to-behavioral-economics.

5   Google Scholar, "Judgment under Uncertainty," accessed April 21, 2016, https://scholar.google.com/scholar?hl=en&q="Judgment+under+Uncertainty"&btnG=&as_sdt=1%2C10&as_sdtp=.

GLOSSARY

GLOSSARY OF TERMS

Adaptive toolbox: the set of tools (including heuristics) used by an individual or group to make decisions. The concept was developed by the German psychologist Gerd Gigerenzer, who argues that our adaptive toolbox is shaped by evolution, learning, and culture.

Anchoring heuristic: a shortcut used in decision-making that begins from psychological starting points, or "anchors"—information that we use as a base from which to assess new information.

Availability heuristic: the idea that people often judge how frequently an event occurs based on how recent, salient (conspicuous or obvious), or accessible it is in our memory.

Bayesian statistics: a means to use probability as a way of quantifying uncertainty. This approach assesses the information we know and then generates a mathematical equation about the probability of an event occurring.

Behavioral economics: the application of scientific insights into human behavior to understanding and predicting our economic decisions.

Behavioral finance: the study of human behavior and psychology involved in financial decision-making.

Behaviorism: a school of thought within psychology that places emphasis on limiting study to objectively observed behavior.

Bias: a systematic deviation from a norm or reference point.

Bounded rationality: the principle that the human decision-making process is limited by the information available, the complexity of the decision, our cognitive limitations, and the time available to make the decision.

Cognition: the mental processes related to thinking, memory, and language.

Cognitive psychology: the study of the human mind and behavior as it relates to thought.

Cognitive revolution: a movement within psychology during the 1950s in which researchers began to focus on how people think, remember, reason, solve problems, and communicate.

Descriptive model of decision-making: a model that aims to describe how decisions are made.

Empirical: related to evidence that can be certified by observation.

Expected utility: "utility" is the value associated with a good or a decision; "expected utility" is the value attached to uncertain outcomes.

Expected utility theory: a theory that asserts that individuals choose possible options on the basis of their expected utility.

Heuristic: A rule of thumb or mental shortcut that we use to solve problems.

Heuristics and biases program: the program initiated by Amos Tversky and Daniel Kahneman, which involves the systematic study of heuristics and biases.

"Homo economicus": the hypothetical "economic man" who operates logically and rationally (and embodies the rational agent model).

Israeli Defense Force: the military forces of Israel.

Knesset: the Israeli parliament.

Measurement theory: theory relating to the measurement and quantification of behavior.

Methodology: refers to the specific process, or method, used to shed light on a research subject.

Neoclassical model of economics: neoclassical economics emerged in the 1860s. As well as considering the concept of utility within economics, it also looks at the perceived value of a good to the consumer.

Neuroscience: an interdisciplinary field that explores the relationship between the brain and behavior.

Normative model of decision-making: a model that aims at finding the "norm"—the reference against which other decisions are compared. Any deviation from the norm is considered to be a mistake.

Nudge theory: a theory that advocates the use of behavioral insights to gently push individuals to adopt positive behaviors.

Prescriptive model of decision-making: a model describing how policies and choices ought to occur to be consistent with maximum utility.

Probability estimation: a means by which the likelihood of a given outcome is predicted.

Prospect theory: a theory, created by Daniel Kahneman and Amos Tversky, describing the way humans make choices under conditions of uncertainty.

Psychoanalysis: a therapeutic and theoretical model pertaining to the nature of the unconscious mind and its role in human behavior.

Psychology: the study of the role of the mind in human behavior.

Psychophysics: the area of psychology that deals with the interaction of physical stimuli and mental processes.

Rational agent: in economics, decision theory, and other fields, a rational agent can always compute the outcomes of any decision and always chooses the option that will bring the biggest benefits.

Rational choice theory: a framework for understanding social and economic behavior. Rational choice theory assumes that people are aware of all outcomes and consistently choose the best outcome.

Representativeness heuristic: a heuristic in which a person judges the nature or identity of other people and things by comparing them to stereotypes.

Rorschach inkblot test: a psychological test in which individuals' interpretation of a series of inkblots are used to assess their personality, motivation, and state of mind.

Russell Sage Foundation: an American foundation that sponsors research in social science.

Social psychology: the study of the role of the mind in social behavior.

Social sciences: the various disciplines, such as sociology and psychology, concerned with understanding the forms and theory of social behavior.

Subconscious: the part of the mind in which behavior is decided according to desires, preferences, prejudices, biases, and so on, of which we are not aware.

Utility: the perceived, subjective value of choices and goods.

World War II: A global military conflict that occurred between 1939 and 1945, fought between the Allies (Great Britain, the Soviet Union, and the United States), and the Axis powers (Germany, Italy, and Japan).

PEOPLE MENTIONED IN THE TEXT

Maurice Félix Charles Allais (1911–2010) was a French economist, and the 1988 winner of the Nobel Memorial Prize in Economics.

Adam Alter (b. 1981) is an American researcher in psychology and economics.

Dan Ariely (b. 1960) is an Israeli American psychologist who is a strong proponent of behavioral economics.

Max H. Bazerman (b. 1955) is Jesse Isidor Straus Professor of Business Administration at Harvard Business School.

Gary Belsky (b. 1961) is an American media consultant who coauthored *Why Smart People Make Big Money Mistakes—And How to Correct Them: Lessons from the Life-Changing Science of Behavioral Economics.*

Colin F. Camerer (b. 1959) is an American behavioral economist.

L. Jonathan Cohen (1923–2006) was a British philosopher who specialized in the power of reasoning.

Tom N. Cornsweet (b. 1929) is an American experimental psychologist, author, inventor, and entrepreneur known for his pioneering work in visual perception and in the development of ophthalmic instrumentation.

Anthony Downs (b. 1930) is an American economist and senior fellow at the Washington DC-based Brookings Institute.

Stephen Dubner (b. 1963) is an American journalist best known for writing *Freakonomics* with the American economist Steven Levitt.★

Ward Edwards (1927–2005) was an American psychologist, best known for his contributions to decision theory.

Hillel J. Einhorn (1941–87) was an American psychologist noted for his research on decision-making. Dr. Einhorn was a professor of behavioral science at the University of Chicago when he died.

Klaus Fiedler (b. 1951) is a German psychologist interested in cognitive social psychology and decision-making. He is a professor of psychology at the University of Heidelberg in Germany.

Milton Friedman (1912 –2006) was an American economist and recipient of the 1976 Nobel Memorial Prize in Economic Sciences.

Barbara Gans is an American psychologist, professor emerita of psychology at Stanford University, and professor of psychology and education at Columbia University. She was Amos Tversky's wife until his death in 1996.

Gerd Gigerenzer (b. 1947) is a German psychologist who directs the Berlin-based Max Planck Institute for Human Development.

Thomas Gilovich (b. 1954) is an American psychologist specializing in decision-making and behavioral economics.

Robin M. Hogarth (b. 1942) is an American psychologist specializing in research on decision-making.

William James (1842–1910) was an American philosopher and psychologist who is often called "the father of American psychology."

George Katona (1901–81) was a Hungarian-born American psychologist who advocated closer connections between the fields of psychology and economics.

John Maynard Keynes (1883–1946) was an influential English economist.

David Isaac Laibson (b. 1966) is an American economist. He is currently professor of economics at Harvard University.

Richard S. Lazarus (1922–2002) was an influential American psychologist, best known for his work on the links between cognition, emotion, and stress.

Steven Levitt (b. 1967) is an American economist and coauthor of the popular 2005 book *Freakonomics*.

Kurt Zadek Lewin (1890–1947) was a German American psychologist considered a pioneer in applied psychology.

Sarah Lichtenstein (b. 1933) is an American psychologist who specializes in judgment and decision-making.

George Loewenstein (b. 1955) is an American economist working in the field of behavioral economics.

Paul Everett Meehl (1920–2003) was an American psychology professor.

Angela Dorothea Merkel (b. 1954) is a German politician and former research scientist. She has been the chancellor of Germany since 2005.

Walter Mischel (b. 1930) is an American psychologist who specializes in personality and social psychology. He is currently professor of psychology at Columbia University.

Don A. Moore is an American psychologist currently serving as an associate professor in the University of California, Berkeley's Haas School of Business.

Barack Hussein Obama II (b. 1961) is the 44th president of the United States.

David A. Rapaport (1911–60) was a Hungarian psychologist who specialized in psychoanalysis.

Norbert Schwarz (b. 1953) is a German psychologist who researches attitude formation and judgment.

Herbert Simon (1916–2001) was an American political scientist, economist, and social scientist.

Paul Slovic (b. 1938) is an American psychologist who specializes in human judgment, decision-making, and risk analysis.

Adam Smith (1723–90) was an influential Scottish philosopher and economist.

Cass R. Sunstein (b. 1954) is an American legal scholar who has worked in both the political arena and academia.

Richard Thaler (b. 1945) is an American economist known for his contributions to behavioral finance.

Anne Treisman (b. 1935) is an English psychologist currently emeritus James S. McDonnell Distinguished University Professor of Psychology at Princeton University. Treisman married Daniel Kahneman in 1978.

Richard Zeckhauser (b. 1940) is an American economist, currently the Frank P. Ramsey Professor of Political Economy at Harvard University.

WORKS CITED

WORKS CITED

Allais, Maurice. "Le comportement de l'homme rationnel devant le risque: critique des postulats et axiomes de l'école américaine." *Econometrica: Journal of the Econometric Society* 21, no. 4 (1953): 503–46.

Ariely, Dan. *Predictably Irrational: The Hidden Forces That Shape Our Decisions*. Revised and expanded edition. New York: HarperCollins, 2009.

Arrow, K., G. Bower, B. Efron, E. Maccoby, E., and L. Ross. "Memorial Resolution for Amos Tversky." Stanford University. Mimeo. *Stanford Report*, October 16, 2002. Accessed April 25, 2016. http://news.stanford.edu/news/2002/october16/tversky-1016.html.

Bazerman, Max H., and Don. A. Moore. *Judgment in Managerial Decision Making*. New York: Wiley, 2013.

Belsky, Gary, and Thomas Gilovich. *Why Smart People Make Big Money Mistakes and How to Correct Them: Lessons from the Life-Changing Science of Behavioral Economics*. New York: Simon & Schuster, 2010.

Benjamin Jr, Ludy T. "Behavioral Science and the Nobel Prize: A History." *American Psychologist* 58, no. 9 (2003): 731–41.

Camerer, Colin, and George Loewenstein. "Behavioral Economics: Past, Present, Future." In *Advances in Behavioral Economics*, edited by Colin Camerer, George Loewenstein, and Mathew Rabin. Princeton, NJ: Princeton University Press, 2004.

Cohen, L. Jonathan. "On the Psychology of Prediction: Whose is the Fallacy?" *Cognition* 7, no. 4 (1979): 385–407.

———. "Can Human Irrationality be Experimentally Demonstrated?" *Behavioral and Brain Sciences* 4, no. 3 (1981): 317–70.

Downs, Anthony. *An Economic Theory of Democracy.* New York: Harper & Row, 1957.

Economist. "Nudge Nudge, Think Think: The Use of Behavioural Economics in Public Policy Shows Promise," March 24, 2012. Accessed April 21, 2016. http://www.economist.com/node/21551032.

Edwards, Ward. "The Theory of Decision Making." *Psychological Bulletin* 51, no. 4 (1954): 380–417.

———. "Behavioral Decision Theory." *Annual Review of Psychology* 12, no. 1 (1961): 473–98.

———. "Conservatism in Human Information Processing." In *Formal*

Representation of Human Judgment, edited by Benjamin Kleinmuntz, 17–52. New York: John Wiley and Sons, 1968.

Edwards, Ward, Harold Lindman, and Leonard J. Savage. "Bayesian Statistical Inference for Psychological Research." *Psychological Review* 70, no. 3 (1963): 193–242.

Einhorn, Hillel J., and Robin M. Hogarth. "Behavioral Decision Theory: Processes of Judgment and Choice." *Journal of Accounting Research* 19, no. 1 (1981): 1–31.

Fiedler, Klaus, and Momme von Sydow. "Heuristics and Biases: Beyond Tversky and Kahneman's (1974) Judgment under Uncertainty." In *Cognitive Psychology: Revisiting the Classic Studies*, edited by Michael W. Eysenck and David Groome, 146–61. London: Sage Publications, 2015.

Fox, Justin. "From 'Economic Man' to Behavioral Economics." *Harvard Business Review*, May 2015. Accessed April 21, 2016. https://hbr.org/2015/05/from-economic-man-to-behavioral-economics.

Freeman, Karen. "Amos Tversky, Expert on Decision Making, Is Dead at 59." *New York Times*, June 6, 1996. Accessed April 21, 2016. http://www.nytimes.com/1996/06/06/us/amos-tversky-expert-on-decision-making-is-dead-at-59.html.

Gigerenzer, Gerd. "On Narrow Norms and Vague Heuristics: A Reply to Kahneman and Tversky." *Psychological Review* 103, no. 3 (1996): 592–6.

— — —. "The Adaptive Toolbox." In *Bounded Rationality: The Adaptive Toolbox*, edited by G. Gigerenzer and R. Selten, 37–50. Cambridge, MA: MIT Press, 2001.

Gilovich, Thomas, Dale Griffin, and Daniel Kahneman. *Heuristics and Biases: The Psychology of Intuitive Judgment*. Cambridge: Cambridge University Press, 2002.

Gladwell, M. *David and Goliath: Underdogs, Misfits, and the Art of Battling Giants*. New York: Little, Brown and Company, 2013.

Heukelom, Floris. "Kahneman and Tversky and the Origin of Behavioral Economics." Tinbergen Institute Discussion Paper TI 2007–003/1 (2007).

Holt, Jim. "Two Brains Running." *New York Times*, November 25, 2011. Accessed April 21, 2016. http://www.nytimes.com/2011/11/27/books/review/thinking-fast-and-slow-by-daniel-kahneman-book-review.html?_r=0.

Jones, Kitty S. "Cameron's Nudge that Knocked Democracy Down: Mind the Mindspace." Politics and Insights, December 17, 2014. Accessed April 21, 2016. https://kittysjones.wordpress.com/2014/12/17/camerons-nudge-that-knocked-democracy-down-mind-the-mindspace/.

Kahneman, Daniel. "Experiences of Collaborative Research." *American Psychologist* 58, no. 9 (2003): 723–30.

———. *Thinking, Fast and Slow*. New York: Farrar, Strauss and Giroux, 2011.

———. "Behavioural Economics and Public Policy." *Financial Times*, March 21, 2014. Accessed April 25, 2016. https://next.ft.com/content/9d7d31a4-aea8-11e3-aaa6-00144feab7de.

"Daniel Kahneman—Biographical." Nobelprize.org. Accessed April 21, 2016. http://www.nobelprize.org/nobel_prizes/economic-sciences/laureates/2002/kahneman-bio.html.

Kahneman, Daniel, and Shane Frederick. "Representativeness Revisited: Attribute Substitution in Intuitive Judgment." In *Heuristics and Biases: The Psychology of Intuitive Judgment*, edited by Thomas Gilovich, Dale Griffin, and Daniel Kahneman, 49–81. New York: Cambridge University Press, 2002.

Kahneman, Daniel, and Amos Tversky. "On the Interpretation of Intuitive Probability: A Reply to Jonathan Cohen." *Cognition* 7, no. 4 (1979): 409–11.

———. "Prospect Theory: An Analysis of Decision under Risk." *Econometrica: Journal of the Econometric Society* 47, no. 2 (1979): 263–91.

———. "Choices, Values, and Frames." *American Psychologist* 39, no. 4 (1984): 341–50.

———. "On the Reality of Cognitive Illusions." *Psychological Review* 103, no. 3 (1996): 582–91.

Katona, George. *Psychological Analysis of Economic Behavior*. New York: McGraw-Hill, 1951.

Krugman, Paul. "Who Was Milton Friedman?" *New York Review of Books*, February 15, 2007. Accessed April 21, 2016. http://www.nybooks.com/articles/2007/02/15/who-was-milton-friedman/.

Laibson, David, and Richard Zeckhauser. "Amos Tversky and the Ascent of Behavioral Economics." *Journal of Risk and Uncertainty* 16, no. 1 (1998): 7–47.

Lehrer, Jonah. "Milton Friedman and the Rational-Agent Model." *Science Blogs*, January 29, 2007. Accessed April 21, 2016. http://scienceblogs.com/cortex/2007/01/29/milton-friedman-and-the-ration/.

Levitt, Steven D., and Stephen J. Dubner. *Freakonomics: A Rogue Economist Explores the Hidden Side of Everything*. New York: William Morrow, 2006.

Levy, Jack S. "Daniel Kahneman: Judgment, Decision, and Rationality." *Political Science & Politics* 35, no. 2 (2002): 271–3.

McKean, Kevin. "Decisions, Decisions." *Discover* (1985): 22–31.

———. "Decisions: Games Minds Play." *Chicago Tribune*, June 23, 1985. Accessed April 21, 2014. http://articles.chicagotribune.com/1985-06-23/features/8502100242_1_route-soldiers-answers.

Meehl, Paul E. *Clinical Versus Statistical Prediction: A Theoretical Analysis and a Review of the Evidence*. Minneapolis: University of Minnesota Press, 1954.

Mullainathan, Sendhil, and Eldar Shafir. *Scarcity: The New Science of Having Less and How It Defines Our Lives*. New York: Picador, 2014.

New World Encyclopaedia. "Amos Tversky." Accessed April 21, 2016. http://www.newworldencyclopedia.org/entry/Amos_Tversky.

Phillips, Lawrence D., and Detlof von Winterfeldt. "Reflections on the Contributions of Ward Edwards to Decision Analysis and Behavioral Research." In *Advances in Decision Analysis,* edited by W. Edwards, R. Miles, and D. von Winterfeldt, 71–80. London: Cambridge University Press, 2007.

Russell Sage Foundation. Behavioral Economics Roundtable. Accessed April 23, 2016. http://www.russellsage.org/research/behavioral-economics/behavioral-economics-roundtable.

Schwarz, Norbert. "Emotion, Cognition, and Decision Making." *Cognition & Emotion* 14, no. 4 (2000): 433–40.

Shafir, Eldar, and Robyn A. LeBoeuf. "Rationality." *Annual Review of Psychology* 53, no. 1 (2002): 491–517.

Simon, Herbert A. "A Behavioral Model of Rational Choice." *Quarterly Journal of Economics* 69, no. 1 (1955): 99–118.

— — —. *Models of Man, Social and Rational*. New York: John Wiley and Sons, 1957.

Slovic, Paul, Baruch Fischhoff, and Sarah Lichtenstein. "Behavioral Decision Theory." *Annual Review of Psychology* 28, no. 1 (1977): 1–39.

Smith, Adam. "The Theory of Moral Sentiments." Library of Economics and Liberty. Accessed April 21, 2016. http://www.econlib.org/library/Smith/smMS1.html.

Thaler, Richard H., and Shlomo Benartzi. "Save More Tomorrow: Using Behavioral Economics to Increase Employee Saving." *Journal of Political Economy* 112, no. 1 (2004): S164–S187.

Thaler, Richard H., and Cass. R. Sunstein. *Nudge*. New Haven, CT: Yale University Press, 2008.

Tversky, Amos, and Daniel Kahneman. "Judgment under Uncertainty: Heuristics and Biases." *Science* 185, no. 4157 (1974): 1124–31.

— — —. "The Framing of Decisions and the Psychology of Choice." *Science* 211, no. 4481 (1981): 453–8.

Wilke, A., and R. Mata. "Cognitive Bias." In *The Encyclopedia of Human Behavior*, edited by V. S. Ramachandran, vol. 1, 531–5. Cambridge, MA: Academic Press, 2012.

THE MACAT LIBRARY
BY DISCIPLINE

AFRICANA STUDIES

Chinua Achebe's *An Image of Africa: Racism in Conrad's Heart of Darkness*
W. E. B. Du Bois's *The Souls of Black Folk*
Zora Neale Huston's *Characteristics of Negro Expression*
Martin Luther King Jr's *Why We Can't Wait*
Toni Morrison's *Playing in the Dark: Whiteness in the American Literary Imagination*

ANTHROPOLOGY

Arjun Appadurai's *Modernity at Large: Cultural Dimensions of Globalisation*
Philippe Ariès's *Centuries of Childhood*
Franz Boas's *Race, Language and Culture*
Kim Chan & Renée Mauborgne's *Blue Ocean Strategy*
Jared Diamond's *Guns, Germs & Steel: the Fate of Human Societies*
Jared Diamond's *Collapse: How Societies Choose to Fail or Survive*
E. E. Evans-Pritchard's *Witchcraft, Oracles and Magic Among the Azande*
James Ferguson's *The Anti-Politics Machine*
Clifford Geertz's *The Interpretation of Cultures*
David Graeber's *Debt: the First 5000 Years*
Karen Ho's *Liquidated: An Ethnography of Wall Street*
Geert Hofstede's *Culture's Consequences: Comparing Values, Behaviors, Institutes and Organizations across Nations*
Claude Lévi-Strauss's *Structural Anthropology*
Jay Macleod's *Ain't No Makin' It: Aspirations and Attainment in a Low-Income Neighborhood*
Saba Mahmood's *The Politics of Piety: The Islamic Revival and the Feminist Subje*ct
Marcel Mauss's *The Gift*

BUSINESS

Jean Lave & Etienne Wenger's *Situated Learning*
Theodore Levitt's *Marketing Myopia*
Burton G. Malkiel's *A Random Walk Down Wall Street*
Douglas McGregor's *The Human Side of Enterprise*
Michael Porter's *Competitive Strategy: Creating and Sustaining Superior Performance*
John Kotter's *Leading Change*
C. K. Prahalad & Gary Hamel's *The Core Competence of the Corporation*

CRIMINOLOGY

Michelle Alexander's *The New Jim Crow: Mass Incarceration in the Age of Colorblindness*
Michael R. Gottfredson & Travis Hirschi's *A General Theory of Crime*
Richard Herrnstein & Charles A. Murray's *The Bell Curve: Intelligence and Class Structure in American Life*
Elizabeth Loftus's *Eyewitness Testimony*
Jay Macleod's *Ain't No Makin' It: Aspirations and Attainment in a Low-Income Neighborhood*
Philip Zimbardo's *The Lucifer Effect*

ECONOMICS

Janet Abu-Lughod's *Before European Hegemony*
Ha-Joon Chang's *Kicking Away the Ladder*
David Brion Davis's *The Problem of Slavery in the Age of Revolution*
Milton Friedman's *The Role of Monetary Policy*
Milton Friedman's *Capitalism and Freedom*
David Graeber's *Debt: the First 5000 Years*
Friedrich Hayek's *The Road to Serfdom*
Karen Ho's *Liquidated: An Ethnography of Wall Street*

John Maynard Keynes's *The General Theory of Employment, Interest and Money*
Charles P. Kindleberger's *Manias, Panics and Crashes*
Robert Lucas's *Why Doesn't Capital Flow from Rich to Poor Countries?*
Burton G. Malkiel's *A Random Walk Down Wall Street*
Thomas Robert Malthus's *An Essay on the Principle of Population*
Karl Marx's *Capital*
Thomas Piketty's *Capital in the Twenty-First Century*
Amartya Sen's *Development as Freedom*
Adam Smith's *The Wealth of Nations*
Nassim Nicholas Taleb's *The Black Swan: The Impact of the Highly Improbable*
Amos Tversky's & Daniel Kahneman's *Judgment under Uncertainty: Heuristics and Biases*
Mahbub Ul Haq's *Reflections on Human Development*
Max Weber's *The Protestant Ethic and the Spirit of Capitalism*

FEMINISM AND GENDER STUDIES

Judith Butler's *Gender Trouble*
Simone De Beauvoir's *The Second Sex*
Michel Foucault's *History of Sexuality*
Betty Friedan's *The Feminine Mystique*
Saba Mahmood's *The Politics of Piety: The Islamic Revival and the Feminist Subject*
Joan Wallach Scott's *Gender and the Politics of History*
Mary Wollstonecraft's *A Vindication of the Rights of Woman*
Virginia Woolf's *A Room of One's Own*

GEOGRAPHY

The Brundtland Report's *Our Common Future*
Rachel Carson's *Silent Spring*
Charles Darwin's *On the Origin of Species*
James Ferguson's *The Anti-Politics Machine*
Jane Jacobs's *The Death and Life of Great American Cities*
James Lovelock's *Gaia: A New Look at Life on Earth*
Amartya Sen's *Development as Freedom*
Mathis Wackernagel & William Rees's *Our Ecological Footprint*

HISTORY

Janet Abu-Lughod's *Before European Hegemony*
Benedict Anderson's *Imagined Communities*
Bernard Bailyn's *The Ideological Origins of the American Revolution*
Hanna Batatu's *The Old Social Classes And The Revolutionary Movements Of Iraq*
Christopher Browning's *Ordinary Men: Reserve Police Batallion 101 and the Final Solution in Poland*
Edmund Burke's *Reflections on the Revolution in France*
William Cronon's *Nature's Metropolis: Chicago And The Great West*
Alfred W. Crosby's *The Columbian Exchange*
Hamid Dabashi's *Iran: A People Interrupted*
David Brion Davis's *The Problem of Slavery in the Age of Revolution*
Nathalie Zemon Davis's *The Return of Martin Guerre*
Jared Diamond's *Guns, Germs & Steel: the Fate of Human Societies*
Frank Dikotter's *Mao's Great Famine*
John W Dower's *War Without Mercy: Race And Power In The Pacific War*
W. E. B. Du Bois's *The Souls of Black Folk*
Richard J. Evans's *In Defence of History*
Lucien Febvre's *The Problem of Unbelief in the 16th Century*
Sheila Fitzpatrick's *Everyday Stalinism*

Eric Foner's *Reconstruction: America's Unfinished Revolution, 1863-1877*
Michel Foucault's *Discipline and Punish*
Michel Foucault's *History of Sexuality*
Francis Fukuyama's *The End of History and the Last Man*
John Lewis Gaddis's *We Now Know: Rethinking Cold War History*
Ernest Gellner's *Nations and Nationalism*
Eugene Genovese's *Roll, Jordan, Roll: The World the Slaves Made*
Carlo Ginzburg's *The Night Battles*
Daniel Goldhagen's *Hitler's Willing Executioners*
Jack Goldstone's *Revolution and Rebellion in the Early Modern World*
Antonio Gramsci's *The Prison Notebooks*
Alexander Hamilton, John Jay & James Madison's *The Federalist Papers*
Christopher Hill's *The World Turned Upside Down*
Carole Hillenbrand's *The Crusades: Islamic Perspectives*
Thomas Hobbes's *Leviathan*
Eric Hobsbawm's *The Age Of Revolution*
John A. Hobson's *Imperialism: A Study*
Albert Hourani's *History of the Arab Peoples*
Samuel P. Huntington's *The Clash of Civilizations and the Remaking of World Order*
C. L. R. James's *The Black Jacobins*
Tony Judt's *Postwar: A History of Europe Since 1945*
Ernst Kantorowicz's *The King's Two Bodies: A Study in Medieval Political Theology*
Paul Kennedy's *The Rise and Fall of the Great Powers*
Ian Kershaw's *The "Hitler Myth": Image and Reality in the Third Reich*
John Maynard Keynes's *The General Theory of Employment, Interest and Money*
Charles P. Kindleberger's *Manias, Panics and Crashes*
Martin Luther King Jr's *Why We Can't Wait*
Henry Kissinger's *World Order: Reflections on the Character of Nations and the Course of History*
Thomas Kuhn's *The Structure of Scientific Revolutions*
Georges Lefebvre's *The Coming of the French Revolution*
John Locke's *Two Treatises of Government*
Niccolò Machiavelli's *The Prince*
Thomas Robert Malthus's *An Essay on the Principle of Population*
Mahmood Mamdani's *Citizen and Subject: Contemporary Africa And The Legacy Of Late Colonialism*
Karl Marx's *Capital*
Stanley Milgram's *Obedience to Authority*
John Stuart Mill's *On Liberty*
Thomas Paine's *Common Sense*
Thomas Paine's *Rights of Man*
Geoffrey Parker's *Global Crisis: War, Climate Change and Catastrophe in the Seventeenth Century*
Jonathan Riley-Smith's *The First Crusade and the Idea of Crusading*
Jean-Jacques Rousseau's *The Social Contract*
Joan Wallach Scott's *Gender and the Politics of History*
Theda Skocpol's *States and Social Revolutions*
Adam Smith's *The Wealth of Nations*
Timothy Snyder's *Bloodlands: Europe Between Hitler and Stalin*
Sun Tzu's *The Art of War*
Keith Thomas's *Religion and the Decline of Magic*
Thucydides's *The History of the Peloponnesian War*
Frederick Jackson Turner's *The Significance of the Frontier in American History*
Odd Arne Westad's *The Global Cold War: Third World Interventions And The Making Of Our Times*

LITERATURE

Chinua Achebe's *An Image of Africa: Racism in Conrad's Heart of Darkness*
Roland Barthes's *Mythologies*
Homi K. Bhabha's *The Location of Culture*
Judith Butler's *Gender Trouble*
Simone De Beauvoir's *The Second Sex*
Ferdinand De Saussure's *Course in General Linguistics*
T. S. Eliot's *The Sacred Wood: Essays on Poetry and Criticism*
Zora Neale Huston's *Characteristics of Negro Expression*
Toni Morrison's *Playing in the Dark: Whiteness in the American Literary Imagination*
Edward Said's *Orientalism*
Gayatri Chakravorty Spivak's *Can the Subaltern Speak?*
Mary Wollstonecraft's *A Vindication of the Rights of Women*
Virginia Woolf's *A Room of One's Own*

PHILOSOPHY

Elizabeth Anscombe's *Modern Moral Philosophy*
Hannah Arendt's *The Human Condition*
Aristotle's *Metaphysics*
Aristotle's *Nicomachean Ethics*
Edmund Gettier's *Is Justified True Belief Knowledge?*
Georg Wilhelm Friedrich Hegel's *Phenomenology of Spirit*
David Hume's *Dialogues Concerning Natural Religion*
David Hume's *The Enquiry for Human Understanding*
Immanuel Kant's *Religion within the Boundaries of Mere Reason*
Immanuel Kant's *Critique of Pure Reason*
Søren Kierkegaard's *The Sickness Unto Death*
Søren Kierkegaard's *Fear and Trembling*
C. S. Lewis's *The Abolition of Man*
Alasdair MacIntyre's *After Virtue*
Marcus Aurelius's *Meditations*
Friedrich Nietzsche's *On the Genealogy of Morality*
Friedrich Nietzsche's *Beyond Good and Evil*
Plato's *Republic*
Plato's *Symposium*
Jean-Jacques Rousseau's *The Social Contract*
Gilbert Ryle's *The Concept of Mind*
Baruch Spinoza's *Ethics*
Sun Tzu's *The Art of War*
Ludwig Wittgenstein's *Philosophical Investigations*

POLITICS

Benedict Anderson's *Imagined Communities*
Aristotle's *Politics*
Bernard Bailyn's *The Ideological Origins of the American Revolution*
Edmund Burke's *Reflections on the Revolution in France*
John C. Calhoun's *A Disquisition on Government*
Ha-Joon Chang's *Kicking Away the Ladder*
Hamid Dabashi's *Iran: A People Interrupted*
Hamid Dabashi's *Theology of Discontent: The Ideological Foundation of the Islamic Revolution in Iran*
Robert Dahl's *Democracy and its Critics*
Robert Dahl's *Who Governs?*
David Brion Davis's *The Problem of Slavery in the Age of Revolution*

Alexis De Tocqueville's *Democracy in America*
James Ferguson's *The Anti-Politics Machine*
Frank Dikotter's *Mao's Great Famine*
Sheila Fitzpatrick's *Everyday Stalinism*
Eric Foner's *Reconstruction: America's Unfinished Revolution, 1863-1877*
Milton Friedman's *Capitalism and Freedom*
Francis Fukuyama's *The End of History and the Last Man*
John Lewis Gaddis's *We Now Know: Rethinking Cold War History*
Ernest Gellner's *Nations and Nationalism*
David Graeber's *Debt: the First 5000 Years*
Antonio Gramsci's *The Prison Notebooks*
Alexander Hamilton, John Jay & James Madison's *The Federalist Papers*
Friedrich Hayek's *The Road to Serfdom*
Christopher Hill's *The World Turned Upside Down*
Thomas Hobbes's *Leviathan*
John A. Hobson's *Imperialism: A Study*
Samuel P. Huntington's *The Clash of Civilizations and the Remaking of World Order*
Tony Judt's *Postwar: A History of Europe Since 1945*
David C. Kang's *China Rising: Peace, Power and Order in East Asia*
Paul Kennedy's *The Rise and Fall of Great Powers*
Robert Keohane's *After Hegemony*
Martin Luther King Jr.'s *Why We Can't Wait*
Henry Kissinger's *World Order: Reflections on the Character of Nations and the Course of History*
John Locke's *Two Treatises of Government*
Niccolò Machiavelli's *The Prince*
Thomas Robert Malthus's *An Essay on the Principle of Population*
Mahmood Mamdani's *Citizen and Subject: Contemporary Africa And The Legacy Of Late Colonialism*
Karl Marx's *Capital*
John Stuart Mill's *On Liberty*
John Stuart Mill's *Utilitarianism*
Hans Morgenthau's *Politics Among Nations*
Thomas Paine's *Common Sense*
Thomas Paine's *Rights of Man*
Thomas Piketty's *Capital in the Twenty-First Century*
Robert D. Putman's *Bowling Alone*
John Rawls's *Theory of Justice*
Jean-Jacques Rousseau's *The Social Contract*
Theda Skocpol's *States and Social Revolutions*
Adam Smith's *The Wealth of Nations*
Sun Tzu's *The Art of War*
Henry David Thoreau's *Civil Disobedience*
Thucydides's *The History of the Peloponnesian War*
Kenneth Waltz's *Theory of International Politics*
Max Weber's *Politics as a Vocation*
Odd Arne Westad's *The Global Cold War: Third World Interventions And The Making Of Our Times*

POSTCOLONIAL STUDIES

Roland Barthes's *Mythologies*
Frantz Fanon's *Black Skin, White Masks*
Homi K. Bhabha's *The Location of Culture*
Gustavo Gutiérrez's *A Theology of Liberation*
Edward Said's *Orientalism*
Gayatri Chakravorty Spivak's *Can the Subaltern Speak?*

PSYCHOLOGY

Gordon Allport's *The Nature of Prejudice*
Alan Baddeley & Graham Hitch's *Aggression: A Social Learning Analysis*
Albert Bandura's *Aggression: A Social Learning Analysis*
Leon Festinger's *A Theory of Cognitive Dissonance*
Sigmund Freud's *The Interpretation of Dreams*
Betty Friedan's *The Feminine Mystique*
Michael R. Gottfredson & Travis Hirschi's *A General Theory of Crime*
Eric Hoffer's *The True Believer: Thoughts on the Nature of Mass Movements*
William James's *Principles of Psychology*
Elizabeth Loftus's *Eyewitness Testimony*
A. H. Maslow's *A Theory of Human Motivation*
Stanley Milgram's *Obedience to Authority*
Steven Pinker's *The Better Angels of Our Nature*
Oliver Sacks's *The Man Who Mistook His Wife For a Hat*
Richard Thaler & Cass Sunstein's *Nudge: Improving Decisions About Health, Wealth and Happiness*
Amos Tversky's *Judgment under Uncertainty: Heuristics and Biases*
Philip Zimbardo's *The Lucifer Effect*

SCIENCE

Rachel Carson's *Silent Spring*
William Cronon's *Nature's Metropolis: Chicago And The Great West*
Alfred W. Crosby's *The Columbian Exchange*
Charles Darwin's *On the Origin of Species*
Richard Dawkin's *The Selfish Gene*
Thomas Kuhn's *The Structure of Scientific Revolutions*
Geoffrey Parker's *Global Crisis: War, Climate Change and Catastrophe in the Seventeenth Century*
Mathis Wackernagel & William Rees's *Our Ecological Footprint*

SOCIOLOGY

Michelle Alexander's *The New Jim Crow: Mass Incarceration in the Age of Colorblindness*
Gordon Allport's *The Nature of Prejudice*
Albert Bandura's *Aggression: A Social Learning Analysis*
Hanna Batatu's *The Old Social Classes And The Revolutionary Movements Of Iraq*
Ha-Joon Chang's *Kicking Away the Ladder*
W. E. B. Du Bois's *The Souls of Black Folk*
Émile Durkheim's *On Suicide*
Frantz Fanon's *Black Skin, White Masks*
Frantz Fanon's *The Wretched of the Earth*
Eric Foner's *Reconstruction: America's Unfinished Revolution, 1863-1877*
Eugene Genovese's *Roll, Jordan, Roll: The World the Slaves Made*
Jack Goldstone's *Revolution and Rebellion in the Early Modern World*
Antonio Gramsci's *The Prison Notebooks*
Richard Herrnstein & Charles A Murray's *The Bell Curve: Intelligence and Class Structure in American Life*
Eric Hoffer's *The True Believer: Thoughts on the Nature of Mass Movements*
Jane Jacobs's *The Death and Life of Great American Cities*
Robert Lucas's *Why Doesn't Capital Flow from Rich to Poor Countries?*
Jay Macleod's *Ain't No Makin' It: Aspirations and Attainment in a Low Income Neighborhood*
Elaine May's *Homeward Bound: American Families in the Cold War Era*
Douglas McGregor's *The Human Side of Enterprise*
C. Wright Mills's *The Sociological Imagination*

Thomas Piketty's *Capital in the Twenty-First Century*
Robert D. Putman's *Bowling Alone*
David Riesman's *The Lonely Crowd: A Study of the Changing American Character*
Edward Said's *Orientalism*
Joan Wallach Scott's *Gender and the Politics of History*
Theda Skocpol's *States and Social Revolutions*
Max Weber's *The Protestant Ethic and the Spirit of Capitalism*

THEOLOGY

Augustine's *Confessions*
Benedict's *Rule of St Benedict*
Gustavo Gutiérrez's *A Theology of Liberation*
Carole Hillenbrand's *The Crusades: Islamic Perspectives*
David Hume's *Dialogues Concerning Natural Religion*
Immanuel Kant's *Religion within the Boundaries of Mere Reason*
Ernst Kantorowicz's *The King's Two Bodies: A Study in Medieval Political Theology*
Søren Kierkegaard's *The Sickness Unto Death*
C. S. Lewis's *The Abolition of Man*
Saba Mahmood's *The Politics of Piety: The Islamic Revival and the Feminist Subject*
Baruch Spinoza's *Ethics*
Keith Thomas's *Religion and the Decline of Magic*

COMING SOON

Chris Argyris's *The Individual and the Organisation*
Seyla Benhabib's *The Rights of Others*
Walter Benjamin's *The Work Of Art in the Age of Mechanical Reproduction*
John Berger's *Ways of Seeing*
Pierre Bourdieu's *Outline of a Theory of Practice*
Mary Douglas's *Purity and Danger*
Roland Dworkin's *Taking Rights Seriously*
James G. March's *Exploration and Exploitation in Organisational Learning*
Ikujiro Nonaka's *A Dynamic Theory of Organizational Knowledge Creation*
Griselda Pollock's *Vision and Difference*
Amartya Sen's *Inequality Re-Examined*
Susan Sontag's *On Photography*
Yasser Tabbaa's *The Transformation of Islamic Art*
Ludwig von Mises's *Theory of Money and Credit*

Printed in the United States
by Baker & Taylor Publisher Services